My Weekly

2024 ANNUAL

PAGE
24

PAGE
48

PAGE
102

FICTION

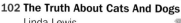

CELEBRITY

COOKERY

BRAINBOOSTERS

THE STARS WHO INSPIRE US

We are in awe of Jane McDonald, who went from a shy youngster to realising her dreams as a singing superstar!

When Jane McDonald first appeared on the BBC1 docusoap *The Cruise* back in 1998, little did she know it would be the start of a showbiz career that would see her loved by millions.

Emerging from the show, which was watched by 13 million viewers at its peak, Jane's first album outsold her nearest rivals by four to one and remained at the top of the chards for three weeks. Her subsequent albums have proven to be a success too and she's never too far from

the stage or screen, where her bubbly personality and powerful voice continue to entertain and enthral.

Jane wasn't always the confident, superstar singer and actor she is today. In her autobiography *Riding the Waves: My Story*, Jane describes herself as a painfully shy child, "fearful of the world beyond our front door". But her grandmother made a psychic prediction of Jane's future, saying, "There are wheels: there are cars, trains and planes. You're going everywhere, you're going all over the world." Her granddaughter became famous when she appeared on *The Cruise*, as she criss-crossed the oceans, and has since travelled widely with her touring and television work.

Jane's beloved late mother Jean also had a clear vision for her daughter's future and became the person who most influenced her life. "And still does, to this day," Jane says. "Because everything she taught me, I still live by. I was very blessed to have her as my mum and my confidante and my person who guided, not pushed. She knew me better than anyone. She was kind, she was fabulous, and I miss her."

Her family had faith in her and sure enough, Jane's beautiful voice and winning personality inspired her to huge success. We're very glad she found her voice! ➡

Just like the lovely Jane, these stars have also taken their talents to great heights...

MIRIAM MARGOLYES

There's personality, then there's personality, then there's Miriam Margolyes! We love her no-nonsense attitude, rather frank approach to life, and of course her amazing – and sometimes X-rated – sense of humour! The actor needs no introduction for her decades of critical acclaim and hundreds of roles across stage and screen, but in recent times she has become as famous for her outspoken approach to life and her tendency to call a spade a spade. Miriam has talked about many issues including feminism, sexuality, politics and more and whatever she has to say, we always want to listen!

OLIVIA COLMAN

After making a name for herself as a comic actor, Olivia's versatility quickly became apparent as she found herself the go-to actor for all sorts of varied roles, playing everyone from a hard-bitten detective in *Broadchurch* to Her Majesty the Queen in the Netflix smash *The Crown*. Of course, many will know her for her wonderfully endearing speech when she won an Oscar in 2019 for *The Favourite*. She also won a lot of respect for wearing a statement ring at the Golden Globes in 2020 which said "Equal Representation For Actresses". She's a star in every sense of the word!

NADIYA HUSSAIN

We all fell in love with Nadiya in 2015 when she became the winner of the sixth series of *The Great British Bake Off*. Her warmth, humour, and yes her skills in the famous kitchen, endeared her to the TV audience, but that triumph was only the beginning. Since then she has become a huge star with books, TV shows, tours and much more. As well as her culinary skills, we also admire Nadiya for speaking frankly about mental health issues and the challenges they bring as she balances a busy career and family life. Through it all her smile is never far away. ➜

ANNEKA RICE

For more than three decades, the intrepid and inspiring Anneka Rice has been helping people through her TV shows. After making her name on *Treasure Hunt,* the presenter moved into the eponymous *Challenge Anneka* role which saw her fulfil tasks, challenges and more, all of which served to make life better for individuals and communities. Her kindness and energy shine through, and that is a powerful combination!

ROBSON GREEN

After hitting the height of TV stardom in *Soldier Soldier*, and enjoying chart-topping success with his co-star Jerome Flynn, Robson found the level of fame difficult to cope with and struggled with alcohol. When his counsellor suggested he needed to find something that truly made him happy, he did – fishing! The therapeutic benefits helped the star turn his life around, but also gave him the inspiration to try something new in his career. Since then, his fishing documentaries have become TV gold.

SHIRLEY BALLAS

Strictly's head judge is an authority on all matters dance. After winning awards and wowing audiences on the dancefloor herself, she became the go-to person when films or TV shows were being made that required dancing expertise. Among the many famous people she has coached is none other than Hollywood legend Tom Cruise, who was apparently a star pupil! As the leader of the judging panel, Shirley has mastered the art of constructive criticism, giving advice and critiques when they are needed most. There is no doubt Shirley has made the most of the talents she has been given!

Make A Wish

New Year and fireballs… would they help Finty's wish
come true – to stay here in her dream home?

By Tess Niland Kimber

"There! What do you think?" Dion beamed at Finty as he tightened the last handle on the kitchen unit.

"Wow! It's gorgeous," she smiled, looking up from her laptop.

Finty gazed around the room, marvelling at the transformation. Who'd think just three weeks ago, this room had housed eight rickety pine units, dated terracotta floor tiles and a dreary Formica dining table.

"I take it you like it then?" Dion said, curling his arms around her.

"It's beautiful. You're so good at this," she smiled, leaning against his shoulder.

"Thank you. It's what I do. As long as you're happy," he kisse her forehead. "Come New Year we'll put the cottage on the market and move on again."

"Um," she said.

"That's the plan, isn't it? Do this up, sell it, buy another and do it all again."

"I suppose," she said.

usually at auction, live in it while they were improving it then sell at a profit.

"One day we'll be able to afford to buy a property outright. Then we can live in it for good," he'd say.

Their plan fitted perfectly with her own homebased business. She'd several high-profile clients who paid her to manage their social media content. She loved it and could work anywhere there was an internet connection. It didn't matter how many different addresses they had in a year. Except that this time it did matter – to Finty. She was getting fed up with constantly moving. More importantly, she didn't want to leave Driftwood cottage.

She gazed around the kitchen. She loved the wealth of dark grey units with the long sweep of oak worktop and the larder in the corner. Normally she couldn't wait to start trawling the estate agent's websites for the next property to renovate but this time was different. Driftwood cottage felt like home, a home she'd always wanted to call her own…

"Let's hope you don't live to regret your decision," her mum had said

He moved away to straighten the striped blind, seemingly unaware his words had robbed her of enthusiasm.

Finty studied him, his broad shoulders, the way his dark hair curled over his collar. He'd worked hard to turn dated, damp, Driftwood cottage into a dream home. He was right; it was what they did. Find a property that needed renovating,

"Driftwood cottage? It's up for sale?"

"Aye," her mum had said back in the summer. "Old Mrs McTaggart has gone to live with her daughter just over the border."

Finty had pulled her mobile from her jeans pocket and looked up the local estate agent website.

"You're right! I wonder if Dion knows?"

Quickly she'd pinged a text to her husband. As she waited for his reply, she thought about Driftwood cottage. She'd always loved it. On Stonehaven harbour, overlooking the North Sea, it was whitewashed with grey painted windows and an oak door.

It would need oodles of work.

Dion had sounded excited when he texted a reply. "Really? Contact Hamish McDonald. Tell him we'll put in an offer."

"Unseen?"

"You know the cottage well enough."

She did as he asked and was delighted when their offer was accepted.

"We've got Driftwood cottage," she'd said, dancing around her mum's kitchen.

"You might not be so happy when you start all the hard work," her mum had said, her blue eyes haunted with concern. "Let's hope you don't live to regret it."

However, Finty loved the cottage and now they owned it, she was certain nothing could go wrong…

Her mum's words echoed through her mind, often. The cottage had needed more work than they'd anticipated – new roof, windows, central heating, a shower room and now this kitchen. Luckily Dion was a builder who could turn his hand to any task and Finty loved working alongside him when she had the time.

"You've learned so much, you're a real help to me," he'd say.

"Bet you tell all your labourers that," she'd grinned.

"Only the ones I'm married to."

It had been Dion's idea to buy properties ripe for renovation and live in them while they worked.

"One day we'll have enough to buy our own wee house outright," he'd say, "but until then we'll keep buying and selling."

Finty agreed but lately that day couldn't come soon enough. To have a home of their own they could live in for good was her dream – especially if it was Driftwood cottage. ➤

"O ch no, Finty," Dion had said when she'd voiced her hopes that they might live in Driftwood after it was finished. "I love the cottage but I dinnae want to live in Stonehaven."

"What's wrong with the village?"

"Nothing," he'd smiled, "But you know me, I love the city. I want to live somewhere lively, like Aberdeen or Dundee."

She'd once agreed, but that was before they'd bought Driftwood cottage. Built to house a fisherman's family at the turn of the last century, the whitewashed cottage oozed charm and now Dion had worked his magic, it had all the benefits of modern living – it was warm, cosy and energy efficient. With three bedrooms it would be perfect for starting a family. And while Dion was right that the village could be a little quiet, especially in winter, it was an ideal area to bring up children. But the city was in Dion's veins. He'd been brought up in Aberdeen and missed it.

"There's always something going on, plenty of nightlife, cinemas, theatres, culture – what more can I say?"

He was right, of course, but there was something about Stonehaven, and about Driftwood cottage, that had seeped into Finty's heart.

C hristmas had been wonderful. Not only had her parents come to them but they'd also had her best friend Hannah and her boyfriend Cameron to visit.

"Wow! What a beautiful cottage," Hannah had exclaimed when they arrived.

Dion had taken the cases from her. "Want to buy it? It goes up for sale in the New Year."

Finty had shivered and Hannah had noticed. "Sell it? Why would you want to leave somewhere so lovely, and after all your hard work, too?"

"Well, it's what we do, and my eye's already on another property. A two-bed terrace in Dunkeld, in desperate need of some TLC."

"Dunkeld's a lovely spot," Cameron agreed as Dion showed him upstairs to the spare room where they'd stay.

As their footsteps became more distant, Hannah leaned towards Finty and whispered, "I take it you'd rather stay?"

"Aye, I would. I can't bear to leave the cottage – or all that," she said, nodding towards the harbour view from the kitchen window. "But Dion says it's time to move on."

"Driftwood's beautiful, I can see why you want to stay."

"It's not just the cottage. I've grown to love Stonehaven. It's so peaceful. I work well here, and I love the views, the walks and the town. There's always something going on, actually."

Hannah reached for her hands. "Then tell him, tell Dion you want to stay. Maybe there's a way."

T he few days spent with their friends were wonderful but there was little chance for Finty to do as Hannah suggested and speak to Dion about staying in Stonehaven. There had been bracing walks to Dunnottar Castle and along the boardwalk, watching for dolphins bobbing in the North Sea.

"These sculptures are gorgeous," Hannah exclaimed as they passed another stunning piece of nautical steelwork, this time a lighthouse. "Who's the sculptor?"

"They call him Stonehaven Banksy," Finty explained, admiring the outdoor art. "No one is sure who he is. He puts them up under the cover of darkness."

"You know lots about our little village," Dion said, pulling her into his arms.

"Just interested," she said, noting he'd said, *our village*.

Dion raised his eyebrows and was about to speak when Cameron thumped his gloved hands together.

"Come on, let's find a café. Who's for a hot chocolate? On me."

"Wow! The cold must have got to ye, offering to pay," Hannah teased.

Hurrying along the boardwalk they found Coastal, a harbourside café, with a welcoming log burner surrounded by squidgy sofas.

"What a lovely welcome," Dion said, toasting his hands by the fire.

There was a delicious aroma of roasted coffee and Hannah couldn't take her eyes from the homemade cakes under the glass domes on the counter.

"Thank goodness calories don't count off together for Christmas. The hospital will be heaving over New Year."

Finty nodded as they waved goodbye to their friends.

"It was great spending time with them, but I suppose now we're on our own again we ought to start packing, too. Come the New Year, I'll speak to the agent selling the Dunkeld property."

"Must you?" Finty said, quietly. "I love it here. Let's just enjoy Hogmanay before we think of leaving. Remember we've the Fireball Festival to go to."

"Oh yes, I cannae wait. Your mum says it's a real spectacle."

Hogmanay was spent at Finty's parents' home in nearby Cowie but after dinner, they set off for Stonehaven.

"You sure you won't come?" Finty asked her mum.

"Och no, it's minus seven tonight. I love the Fireball Festival but the waiting will finish me off."

They laughed as they said goodbye, wishing them the best for New Year.

"Then tell him – tell him you want to stay. Maybe there's a way," she said

at Christmas," she laughed. A round of hot chocolate topped with marshmallows and cream soon arrived as they sat near the log burner to share homemade mince pies.

"I could get used to this," Dion said, biting into the crisp pastry. Finty caught his eye. Did he mean it? Was Stonehaven working its charm on him, too?

What a shame you can't stay for Hogmanay," Finty said as Cameron and Hannah loaded the car with their cases ready to leave.

"I know but we were lucky to get time

"Take lots of photos," Finty's dad said as they drove away.

As they neared Stonehaven, Dion said, "It seems early to come home."

"Well, Mum says people start gathering from ten o'clock. If the crowd's too big, they close the High Street. We don't want to miss it."

They parked at Driftwood cottage and, holding hands, made their way to town. Finding a spot by the music store, they huddled behind the barriers.

"Look!" Finty said, pointing along the street as a pipe band started to play.

He pretended to cover his ears with ➡

his gloved hands, and she laughed. With tinsel and fairy lights decorating their bagpipes, it was a wonderful sight, but she couldn't wait for the main event.

"I'm freezing," he said, snuggling into her. "I can see why Mum wasn't keen to join us."

Finty was cold too but didn't take too much notice as she was excited for the Fireballs Festival.

"Only moments left of the old year," he amazement, watching as some marchers swung the fireballs using just one arm.

Showers of sparks fell around the walkers as the band struck up *Auld Lang Syne*. The crowd sang, linking arms with their neighbours. Finty loved it. She'd never been to such an unusual Hogmanay. The atmosphere was fantastic.

After marching for about twenty minutes, the walkers made their way to the harbour where they swung the

All this time she'd tried to find the right words to voice her hopes and dreams

whispered. "If 2024 is as good with you as this year, it'll be amazing."

The crowd began the countdown and the Town House bells chimed.

"Five, four, three, two, one! Happy New Year!" everyone shouted as the fireballs – huge wire cages filled with twigs and oily rags – were lit.

Finty made a wish as the last bell chimed, mentally begging to stay at Driftwood. When she opened her eyes, the marchers were swinging the massive balls over their heads.

"Isn't it dangerous?" she asked Dion.

"Och no, the cages are on five-foot long wire ropes," he explained.

Soon there were about fifty people, marching through the town, swinging the huge fireballs high above their heads in a wide circular movement. Despite the freezing cold the men were dressed in traditional kilts.

"The balls are so heavy," Finty said, in flaming balls as high as they could before throwing them into the sea.

The crowd cheered, wishing everyone, "Happy New Year!"

"What an amazing custom," Dion said, clapping the marchers. "Do you know why they do this?"

"No one's sure, but some say there was a shooting star above Stonehaven many years ago one Hogmanay and the following year there were bumper crops in the area. They used fireballs afterwards to imitate the shooting star to ensure future prosperity for the town."

"Well, I hope it brings us luck, too," he said, kissing her. "Happy New Year."

Finty kissed him back, wishing they'd be spending 2024 in Driftwood cottage.

Finty had enjoyed Christmas and New Year, but it was time to get back to work. Dion had set her up a workstation in the third bedroom and she loved to sit at

her desk, looking over the harbour.

As each day passed, she braced herself for her husband to appear with the cardboard boxes, ready to pack for the next move but he didn't seem keen to start. Maybe he found returning to work hard after the long holiday?

The first week passed with Dion busy working on another house in the town for one of their neighbours. One morning she asked him how the purchase of the Dunkeld property was going.

"Oh, there's been a few problems," he confessed. "The owner's thinking about holding onto the property. He might not sell after all."

Her heart soared. Would they get some more time here at Driftwood cottage?

"I suppose we ought to start looking for other properties," she said, dreading the move.

"Um, maybe," he said, before rushing out of the back door.

When January slipped into a very cold February and Dion had still not talked about buying another property, Finty brought it up over a warming dinner of neeps and tatties.

Dion took a deep breath. "Well, I've been wondering if we ought to consider staying here."

"What? In Stonehaven?"

"Yes – but, more importantly, in Driftwood cottage."

"Really?" she beamed, jumping up to sit on his lap.

"You're pleased? You don't mind staying here?" he asked, frowning.

"Mind! I love the idea!" she told him.

"But you've asked me a lot lately about finding a new property. I thought you'd gone off the idea of staying here."

"Never! You've made this my dream home. But how would it work? We've saved a lot over the years but not enough to buy it outright."

"No, that we cannae, but I've been thinking about starting my own building business. I've been offered lots of work in Stonehaven and the surrounding villages."

"So, we can stay here?"

"Yes – with your income alongside the work I've managed to pick up, we can see how it goes."

"And you really don't mind that we'll be settling down in a village rather than in the city?"

"Och, I love the city – always will – but the time's right to live somewhere quiet. For when the bairns start coming along."

She shook her head in disbelief. All this time she'd been trying to find the right words to voice her hopes and dreams, not knowing that he shared them, too.

"What changed your mind?"

He considered for a minute and then said, "The Fireball Festival. Being part of a strong community, I thought, we wouldn't get that in a city. And we wouldn't get that view either."

He nodded towards the harbour and then added, "So, shall we stay?"

"Yes, please!" she said, dipping her head to kiss him, thinking that maybe New Year's wishes really did come true after all. Well, at least in Stonehaven, they did… **MW**

A Lot Of Promise

Treat each day like a gift, for you never know what the future might hold…

By Carrie Hewlett

H ey! What do you think you're doing?" The gruff voice made Bree jump as she tried to wiggle the front door key. Uncle Jack had said it could stick but this was ridiculous.

As she turned her head, she caught a faint whiff of cedarwood and tangerine before the wind caught it and tossed it away like a leaf on a breeze.

"Trying to get in," she said curtly, feeling more like a child being caught with her hands in the cookie jar than a thirty-year old woman.

Her gaze met honey brown eyes infused with green flecks as if soft moss had taken up residence. She could

he's visiting my cousins in Australia, as he wanted someone keeping an eye on the place." She gave the man an icy stare. "And who are you?"

The animosity melted away as the man smiled in surprise, his eyes lighting up in pleasure. "Bree? Gosh, you've changed –

She had enjoyed so many summer holidays here with her wayward uncle

imagine them sparkling with fun, only right now they looked dark and intense as if a storm were approaching.

"And who gave you permission?" The voice was still terse.

Feeling sparks of annoyance Bree squared her shoulders. "Not that it's any of your business, but my Uncle Jack gave me a key. I'm staying in the cottage while

in a good way I hasten to add. I remember you as an impulsive tomboy with scuffed knees and too many freckles." He gave a deep throaty chuckle.

Weird. He sounded as if he knew her, but she didn't recognise him. Unless… a memory stirred of an annoying, skinny lad who enjoyed making fun of the fact she didn't like being splashed in the sea.

"Mike?" He'd definitely filled out in all the right places with a toned muscular physique that was doing funny things to her insides. She felt her cheeks colour and tried to act nonchalant. After all she wasn't about to leap into another romance having not long ago been dumped. Though perhaps it had been a blessing as Steve had turned out to be rather shallow.

The man nodded, brushing a hand through his dark hair. "As I recall, you were a few years younger than me. Jack did say that you'd be coming to stay but I didn't think that was until next week. Are you staying long?"

"Six weeks. Though it depends on whether my firm want me back sooner. I'm a graphics designer."

"Nice." He nodded his approval. "I turned my love of photography into my business – I'm a wildlife photographer."

"Amazing. Uncle Jack told me about your mum. I'm sorry." She looked towards the only other cottage in the vicinity.

"Thanks. I couldn't bear to sell the place so I moved back." His voice was measured though a shadow fell over his face. "Can I give you a hand with your luggage?"

"Thanks." What was the harm? He was just being friendly.

As they entered the cottage, Bree felt a wave of homecoming. She'd enjoyed so many summer holidays staying with her slightly wayward Uncle, who'd always treated each day as if it were an adventure. He'd taught her how to sail, and how to fish. Once they'd even camped out on the beach and grilled a freshly caught mullet, just because he'd said it would be fun. He'd been right. Bree was certain the fish tasted so much ➡

nicer for having been cooked outside.

She'd have to get the heating on pronto. Still, what could you expect? It was late January after all. February was only days away.

As if he'd read her mind, Mike glanced at her. "Do you want a hand with the heating? It's always been a temperamental system. I kept telling Jack he ought to upgrade."

"But I bet he kept saying he'd do it tomorrow! Thanks, that's kind of you."

They both laughed, knowing what her uncle was like at putting certain jobs off.

Mike seemed so different from when she'd come here to stay on holiday. Back then he'd been a bit of a brat, either teasing her or keeping out of her way, but now… She felt her cheeks warm only to see Mike's eyes flash with amusement as he caught her staring as he re-entered the room.

"Any trouble, let me know. The wind does howl around here, especially this time of year."

"I'm sure I'll manage. I'll get settled then drive to the shops for some groceries. Is the path to the beach still passable?"

"Yeah. I go down there most days."

"In which case we might bump into each other." Again she kept her tone light, aware of his strong masculine presence in the small cottage.

"I'm sure we will. And we're due for some heavy rain later, so take care." He smiled warmly. "It's nice to see you, again, Bree."

"You too." If she wasn't mistaken there had definitely been a pull of attraction between them, but it was way too soon for her to fall for someone again.

Determinedly, she closed the door, and looked round her home for the next six weeks. Was it her imagination, or did the cottage seem to almost give a contented sigh, as though it were happy that she was here too? Or was that her subconscious mind giving her a sign that hopeful new beginnings were in the offing?

Over the next few days, Bree found herself settling into a nice routine. She was glad she'd stocked up as Mike was right and the weather took a definite turn for the worse. The wind started wailing around the cottage like a banshee and the heavens opened to a flood of water pouring like a river from the slate grey sky.

She missed getting out into the fresh air, but contented herself with cosying up inside and sketching some new designs.

However, after day four, she itched to be outside. Spotting a patch of blue sky big enough to make a sailor a pair of trousers, as her mum often said, she wrapped up warmly.

With Mike's cottage being directly opposite the path, she couldn't help but see that the place appeared to be in darkness. Not that that was hard; clouds were in silver and black in varying shades of metal hues.

Breathing deep of the briny air, she relished the salty tang on her tongue and the brisk breeze playing with her hair, giving it the same buoyancy as the waves crashing onto the shore.

As she reached the bottom of the pebbled cove, she saw a familiar figure sitting on some nearby rocks, peering through the lens of his camera, obviously intent on getting the right shot. She went to wave, then thought better of it, and started walking in the opposite direction. He was busy and she needed time alone. She recalled her mum's words: *When you find the right one, then you're set up for a life full of love and happiness.* Mums did tend to be right, so, thinking optimistically, who knew what the future might bring?

The bay was small, not much to it really. A few large rocks where Mike sat, and a small expanse of shingle that crunched underfoot as she strode across to the cliff face. Reaching the other side, she lifted her head and shut her eyes, enjoying the sound of land and sea meeting, and the raucous sounds of gulls overhead. She opened her eyes, and stared out across the iron clad waves, lost in her own thoughts, when a deep voice interrupted her.

"Bree… the tide's on the turn."

She turned to see Mike standing beside her, his dark hair plastered to his skull with wetness, and she realised that it had started raining again. He looked up at the storm-tossed clouds overhead. "Unless you want to really become at one with nature, we better get back."

boots, Bree made herself comfortable in one of the grey wingback chairs.

"Have you any plans while you're in the area?" Mike handed her a grey and white china mug.

"Seeing how I feel from day to day." Bree relished the hot liquid after the coolness outside. "Have you never thought of moving?"

He shook his head. "No. I love it here. I much prefer living in solitary with the elements than being surrounded by crowds."

"I can understand that. I'd forgotten how beautiful it was. It's a shame I'm only here for six weeks. Well, five now, I guess."

Was it her imagination or did he look dismayed at her words? With a start she realised she hoped he'd miss her.

Over the next week they continued to meet as friends, and catch up on lost years. Mike enjoyed fishing as much as her, and they both had a love of sea food and a passion for the great outdoors. Besides, she really enjoyed his company.

"I wish I lived closer to the sea," Bree confessed on one of their walks.

Ever since they'd met on the beach, it

They continued to meet up as friends and to catch up on the lost years

They walked in companionable silence, Mike not speaking again until they were at the top of the path. "Fancy a cuppa?"

Should she? But it was only a cup of tea… "OK, thanks."

She'd never set foot in Mike's cottage despite spending many summers with her uncle and cousins. The décor was more modern, with tones of black and cream blending nicely. Once she'd removed her parka, and slipped out of her walking

had seemed natural to hook up, weather permitting. She'd dug out her own camera, not that she was an expert, and together they'd photographed badgers, foxes, and otters, as well as a cute dormouse that Bree nicknamed Pablo for no other reason than it had big brown eyes.

Mike had burst out laughing. "I've never had anyone name something just because of its eye colour before!" ➡

"But it's cute," Bree said, pretending to pout.

Their gaze had met, and she'd seen Mike's eyes darken. Gently, he'd reached out a hand, and tucked a strand of her blonde hair behind one ear with his thumb and forefinger, lightly stroking her neck as he did so, sending spasms of desire flooding through her body.

"You make me see things differently, and I like that."

The blood had coursed through her veins at his touch, but she'd tried to keep her voice light in reply, "Happy to help."

She now knew that without even

sunshine to the bitterly cold day.

"Best I could find and I know yellow is your favourite colour, as you told me."

"Thank you. Is the restaurant far? Only I don't remember seeing anywhere close-by here."

Mike tapped the side of his nose conspiratorially. "It's tucked away behind the hill, but does the best steak and chips I've ever tasted."

They took their seats at a window table in the intimate dining area and Bree gasped in delight at the view overlooking the bay. Fairy lights dotted the landscape, casting a glow across the gunmetal waves

She'd been determined not to fall in love again, but Devon had other ideas

realising it, she'd fallen for him. And when he asked her out to dinner, just before Valentine's Day she'd smiled her acceptance.

"I'm glad you said yes, as I know this lovely place that serves great food."

She was adding a final coat of lipstick when she heard the door, pleased to see Mike's eyes widening in approval.

He passed her a few snowdrops and a couple of yellow winter aconites, that he'd obviously handpicked; the yellow buttercup-like flowers adding a burst of

washing the shore, and stars sprinkled above like dots of glitter in the velvety dark sky. "It's perfect."

The corners of his mouth lifted. "As are you." He gave an apologetic chuckle. "Sorry. Too cheesy?"

She grinned. "Just a bit, but on a night like this, you're allowed."

It still seemed odd. She'd been determined not to fall in love again, but Devon had obviously had other ideas.

Having eaten, Bree sat back feeling replete. "That was superb."

"Room for pudding?"

"I'm not sure."

"Come on," he pressed. "How about we share a chocolate brownie? They're melt in the mouth."

She didn't need much encouragement but still pretended to swoon. "Chocolate? OK, you've found my weakness."

A little later, they meandered down the path towards the beach, his jacket around her shoulders. Taking her hand, his thumb gently caressed the inside of her wrist. "Actually, I've a confession to make."

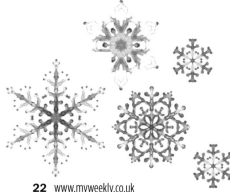

"Oh…" Waves of desire weren't just washing the shore as far as Bree was concerned.

"All those years ago, when I teased you, it wasn't just because you were annoying. There was something else, something that drew me to you, but at the time I just didn't know what."

"And now?" she whispered, feeling hope pierce the air.

He turned to face her, his eyes darkening, his voice having thickened. "Now I'm older and I know different…" He paused, then drew her to him, and Bree melted into his arms.

Valentine's Day dawned clear and bright though she could see dark clouds already gathering. She'd agreed to meet Mike for their usual stroll along the beach, and there was something she needed to tell him…

Although the local shop had a few Valentine's cards, none had seemed quite right so instead Bree had chosen a rather cute card with two dormice, one with big brown eyes. Inside she'd written: *Pablo and…?* followed by a heart.

She met Mike at the top of the path, and they walked down hand in hand before crunching their way across the shingle. Bree could feel the wintry chill cutting through despite her thick clothing.

They took shelter beside the cliff and swapped cards. Mike opened his and chuckled. "Love it."

Opening the one he'd given her Bree saw a familiar photograph: two cottages against a backdrop of a periwinkle blue sky with a heart between them. Her hand flew to her face. "But that's yours and Uncle Jack's…"

"Yes. I've got a contract to provide further photographs to be turned into greetings cards."

"That's brilliant! Congratulations." She hugged him. "And I've got some news of my own. My company have agreed that I can work from home, and just go into the office maybe once or twice a month. Wi-fi is surprisingly good down here, despite coverage not supposing to be the best, and Uncle Jack has asked me to stay on as he's decided to go walkabout in Oz." She grinned as she saw Mike's astonishment. "I know. He always said that we should embrace the moment. Yesterday is history, tomorrow is a mystery, but today's a gift. We just don't always know what it's going to bring."

"He's right." Mike grinned back. "I'm so glad you're staying." He kissed her firmly on the mouth and as Bree wound her arms around his neck, she knew that there was nowhere she'd rather be.

Feeling something wet on her cheek, she glanced up to see snowflakes playfully swirling in the air.

"It's snowing!" She turned delighted eyes to him. "Oh, this is like the icing on the cake!"

"That it is." His arms tightened around her. "Happy Valentine's Day."

"Happy Valentine's Day."

Together they watched the snowflakes dance towards the waves, like feathered crystals. Bree felt like she knew what Uncle Jack meant when he'd said to treat each day like a present and always look forward to tomorrow. She'd taken steps into deep emotional waters, and right now, it was looking as if they held rather a lot of promise. Ⓜ

New Beginnings

Surrounded with primroses and lambs at Easter time, it wasn't long before Flora started to feel at home

By Jan Snook

Flora gazed around Primrose Cottage and felt herself relax.

Her family had stayed in this village every Easter during her childhood, and when she'd seen online that the cottage was to let, she'd signed the lease without a second thought – or even a viewing. She'd picked up the keys that morning, just hours after flying in from New York, and she wasn't regretting it.

She had always loved the tiny cottage, with its quirky thatched roof and higgledy-piggledy garden. At the moment it was living up to its name, with primroses filling every inch of available space.

However she hadn't time to admire the haze of spring-green leaves now. She had jet lag and a lot of unpacking to do

Jake and followed him to New York.

Today, ten whole years later, she was back in Dorset. Alone.

In the prettiest cottage in the most idyllic village in the world, she reminded herself, before she could have doubts about her decision. She had enough money to keep her going for six months, and after that… well, she'd have to see how it went. At least she'd be able to set up her easel and paint, without having to consider whether some pretentious Manhattan gallery would accept her work.

She was free.

Despite her jet lag, Flora lay awake that night, unaccustomed to the unfamiliar silence. When, at last, she drifted off to sleep, she was awoken what seemed like moments later by the dawn

Her heart lifted at the thought of a life of looking up the names of wildflowers

before she could fall into the soft double bed which almost filled the small bedroom tucked under the eaves.

From the eyebrow window she could see Colmer Hill, crowned with its distinctive copse of pine trees. She'd painted it often as a young girl, and it was that view which had later propelled her to art college, where she'd fallen in love with

chorus and the urgent bleating of lambs.

Flora struggled out of bed and drew back the curtains.

In the fields below the hill she could see newborn lambs, their pure white wool a stark contrast to their greyer, well-upholstered mothers. There were clumps of daffodils, and frothy white blossom in the hedgerows. Blackthorn? Maybe, but

she'd have to check. Her heart lifted at the thought of a life which included looking up the names of trees and wildflowers. There'd been no call for it in Central Park.

Ignoring the boxes which needed unpacking, Flora dressed hurriedly and gathered up her paints. She wanted to catch this April morning light.

She set out walking through the village. There was a chilly breeze, and she clutched her jacket more tightly around her, stopping to glance at a poster in the village shop window advertising an Easter Egg Hunt on the green on Easter Saturday – so they were still holding it!

A hundred yards or so further, opposite the village pond (where there had been some dilapidated farm buildings), there was now a smart craft centre. Flora could

see a pottery, a café, and another shop displaying handmade jewellery in the window. Then her eye was caught by what was unmistakably an art gallery.

She took an excited step towards it, but then changed her mind. There'd be plenty of time to explore later.

It took her half an hour to walk up Colmer Hill, and she arrived out of breath. One thing you could say about New York, it was flat. There were already quite a few walkers out, heading into the wind and stopping every now and then to admire the view.

She set up her easel and looked around for some loose stones to act as paperweights to anchor her preliminary sketches once she started to work. ➜

Sheep moved resentfully out of her way, except for one intrepid lamb who was determinedly nibbling a primrose. Soon Flora was engrossed in a world of her own, capturing the lamb in paints.

Although Flora was dimly aware of passing hikers pausing to look over her shoulder while she worked, she was too lost in her composition to take them in. She was on a roll. She'd started three separate paintings, allowing some areas to dry while she worked on others. She worked more and more quickly, desperate to get the colours down before the sun – which had now gone behind a cloud – gave up the ghost altogether.

She saw a passing walker put up the hood of his anorak just as Flora felt the first drops of rain. Time to go.

She'd carefully removed the stone from the first of her pictures and turned to put it in her case, when a sound behind her made her look round.

"I'll help you!" a little boy said delightedly, picking up two more stones.

"No!" she said frantically, but it was too late. The wind had whipped the paintings away, too fast to catch, and both she and the child looked after them wordlessly. They were nowhere in sight.

"Oops!" a man said, running towards them. "You little monkey, Ted! Hope it wasn't anything precious," he added to Flora with a smile. "Kids, eh?" And he and Ted quickly loped off, escaping the rain.

dropped and the sun was shining, so she set out to explore the village.

Despite being Good Friday, most things seemed to be open – presumably for the benefit of the tourists who would be here for the Easter weekend.

She walked past the village shop, which now had buckets of spring flowers outside and, on an impulse, she went in and bought a big bunch of pink tulips.

The craft centre was busier today, and the gallery was open. She quickened her pace but then stopped dead. The window held two delicate paintings on miniature easels: one of a hedgerow and the other of the lamb eating the primroses.

Her paintings.

Anger welled up inside her. How dare someone try to sell her work? She walked inside, seething. Several people were looking at the pictures on the walls, but Flora walked straight up to the desk where a tall man in his thirties was bending over a ledger.

He spoke without looking up. "I'll be with you in a moment, but I'm afraid if you were after the watercolours in the window, they're not for sale."

He put his pen down and straightened up. He had chocolate brown eyes and a smile that made the angry accusations Flora had been formulating evaporate.

"So what can I do for you?" he asked with undisguised interest.

"I did come in about those paintings

She told Toby all about her time in New York with Jake – and about her dreams

When Flora opened the door to her cottage she laid her one remaining painting on the kitchen table, made a cup of tea and concentrated on unpacking all her boxes.

The following day the wind had

in the window," she began, but he interrupted:

"I'm really sorry, but they're not for sale. I wish they were – I could have sold them three times already this morning."

"Where did you get them?" she asked.

"I was walking yesterday, saw them caught in a crevice of a dry stone wall."

"They're mine," Flora said simply. "I was up Colmer Hill yesterday."

He stared at her, then, with dawning recognition, said, "You're Flora, aren't you? We were at art school together. Actually we went out once or twice, but I don't expect you to remember me. That American, Jake, swept you off your feet."

"Toby?" Flora asked doubtfully, and Toby grinned, then called to someone in the back room,

"Hey Colin, can you hold the fort for a mo? I'm going out. Shall I put these in water?" he added, taking the tulips from Flora. "I only live upstairs, and we can collect them later."

It was as if they'd never been apart.

Minutes later Flora and Toby were sitting outside the café next door, gazing at the village pond and sipping cappuccinos.

"Are you sure you're warm enough?" he asked solicitously, but Flora laughed.

"I'm a painter, I'm outside in all weathers," she said, "I'd rather be sitting here admiring the daffodils round the pond than stuck inside, wouldn't you?" second later she added, Oh look! Ducklings! How many has she got?"

"I think it's five… no, six!" Toby said.

"I wish I'd brought my sketchbook, I'd love to draw them," Flora said. "Maybe I'll come out here again later."

"So are you here for long?" Toby asked. "I haven't seen you about."

"Forever, I hope. I flew in from New York on Wednesday – I'm still moving in."

"And…" Toby began hesitantly, "… is Jake with you? Or coming soon?"

"I'm surprised you remember him," Flora said slowly "But no, he's not."

She found herself telling Toby all about her time in New York with Jake, and all about her hopes and impossible dreams.

"So what went wrong?" Toby asked quietly – though not looking displeased.

She smiled wryly.

"Well, Jake was painting huge bold successful canvases of graffiti and skyscrapers, and doing really well, and… well you've seen what I paint. Lambs and wild flowers and rural scenes. I managed to sell enough to make a living, but it was what I sold to greetings card companies that paid the rent."

"Anyone who can make a living painting is doing really well, Flora. You shouldn't be apologetic about it. And as I said, I could have sold those paintings in my window three times already."

"Jake thought my work was twee. I think I embarrassed him. And my paintings were simply too small for New York. Then I discovered he had 'other interests', so I decided to come home…"

Toby reached across the table and put his hand over hers.

Afraid that his sympathy might make her cry, Flora quickly asked, "What's going on over there?" ➡

Toby turned to look.

"Oh, they're getting ready for the Easter Egg Hunt tomorrow. I'll pick you up at eleven, and we'll go together, shall we? There's a parade as well, but I don't suppose you packed your Easter bonnet, did you?" He glanced at his watch and pulled a face, "I ought to get back to the gallery. See you tomorrow!"

Flora went home and picked up her painting things before going straight out again, in search of the ducklings.

The next day Toby arrived promptly at eleven. He was clutching her bunch of tulips, which they'd both forgotten yesterday, and he had clearly added another bunch. Or maybe two.

She took them from him and looked in her kitchen cupboards, trying to remember where she'd put her vases.

"We're meeting my sister Liz and her children there," he began, but then he stopped, his eye caught by the watercolours Flora had laid out on the dresser to dry.

"But these… did you do them after I left you yesterday? They're wonderful," he said, shaking his head in amazement.

She couldn't tell him she painted better when she was happy, and yesterday afternoon she'd been filled with a euphoria she barely recognised.

"This little duckling… it looks as if you could touch the softness of its feathers. And this one of bluebells! There must be thirty shades of blue in there. It's like walking into a wood. You'll have to show it to my mother – she loves bluebells."

He turned to Flora, still shaking his head in wonder. "I was going to ask whether you'd be willing to hold an exhibition in my gallery, but…" He looked embarrassed suddenly, and added, "But of course you'll want to send them to a smart London gallery. I wasn't thinking."

"But I'd love to exhibit in your gallery," Flora said shyly, her heart ballooning in her chest.

The village green, when they arrived for the egg hunt, was a rainbow of pastel bunting, and Liz's children Rosie and Thomas, who were four and six, were bouncing up and down with excitement.

"Look at my bonnet," Rosie gabbled, pointing at her hat which was covered with chicks and eggs and rabbits.

"And mine!" Thomas said. His millinery creation was covered with eggs, chicks and – confusingly – dinosaurs.

Flora admired them extravagantly until it was time for the egg hunt to begin.

At last a huge Easter Bunny blew a whistle and the children rushed around madly, filling their flowery baskets as fast as possible, and managing to cram quite a few eggs into their mouths as they went.

"So are you going to see your family tomorrow?" Liz asked, when there was a lull in the proceedings as Rosie and Thomas were busy demolishing eggs.

For a moment Flora toyed with saying yes to avoid embarrassing them, but instead she shook her head.

"My parents live near Newcastle, and I couldn't face the journey when I still have jet lag. And I haven't finished unpacking."

Toby looked appalled. "You can't spend Easter Sunday on your own! We're all going to our parents' place here in the village. You must come, my mother will be thrilled to have you."

"I can't do that," Flora said, laughing. "I'll be fine, really."

"Yes you can," Toby said, "Otherwise I'll have to come to you and miss my mother's wonderful Easter lunch. You wouldn't do that to me, would you?"

In the end Flora was overruled and, once they'd watched the Easter bonnet parade and clapped loudly as Thomas and Rosie, looking very pleased with themselves, passed, she and Toby walked the few yards to The Fisherman's Arms and had some lunch.

When Toby had gone back to his gallery to relieve Colin, and to "catch the Easter holiday trade", Flora went to the village shop before returning to Primrose Cottage laden with chocolate eggs for the next day. She resisted the

branch, and placed vases and jugs of tulips on every available surface. She looked around in satisfaction: the cottage suddenly looked like home.

Toby's family were as lovely as she had expected. Thomas and Rosie greeted her like a long lost aunt, and Toby's parents seemed genuinely delighted to see her.

"I remember Toby talking about you when he was at college," his mother said, smiling. "I suppose I shouldn't say it, but he had such a crush on you!" she added, making Flora blush. "Now you've moved to our village! That's what Easter's all about, really, isn't it? New beginnings…"

The lunch was delicious. There was roast lamb with new potatoes from the garden, fresh mint sauce and home-made red currant jelly. Later a beautiful Simnel cake appeared, decorated with the traditional marzipan balls, and primroses and violets from the garden.

Then it was time to give out the

"You can't spend Easter Sunday alone! You must come to my mother's house"

urge to go out painting again, and set about making her cottage more habitable – there were still quite a few boxes to unpack. She wouldn't admit, even to herself, that she wanted the cottage to look welcoming for Toby.

She emptied the boxes of books on to the waiting shelves, then went outside to pick a branch of twisted willow which was just coming into leaf, and put it into her last remaining vase.

She opened the last packing box with some trepidation, and was relieved to see that the delicately hand-painted goose eggs inside it had survived the move. Soon she had hung them on the willow

Easter eggs, which the children had been eyeing hungrily since before lunch. Flora distributed the eggs she'd bought, and was embarrassed to receive several in return.

When they had all finished exclaiming over the brightly coloured eggs, Flora handed a flat parcel to Toby's mother, who unwrapped it and stared open-mouthed at the painting of bluebells Flora had framed the previous evening.

"You've all been so kind," Flora said.

Before she could say any more, Toby had taken her into his arms and kissed her rather suddenly.

"To New Beginnings," he said. And kissed her again. Ⓜ

Kriss Kross

Try to fit all the listed words back into the grid.

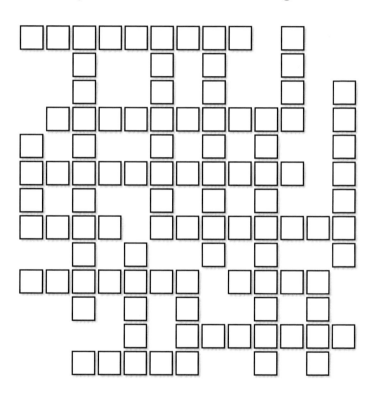

4 letters	5 letters	8 letters	10 letters
EVIL	DRIFT	LOLLIPOP	MEANINGFUL
GALE	UNTIE	POSSIBLE	MEDDLESOME
OGRE	**7 letters**	**9 letters**	**11 letters**
PAGE	GROUPIE	MASCULINE	CATERPILLAR
SCOW	ODYSSEY	NEWSFLASH	SELECTIVITY
WAVE	OUTCROP		

Codeword

Each letter of the alphabet has been replaced by a number. The numbers for the first name of our chosen celebrity are given. Complete the puzzle to reveal which Spice Girl actress Keeley Hawes lived and travelled with for six months during her time at theatre school.

15	18	23	10	11	20	9	25	5	15	19 **K**		2	20	12
16		1		6		11		7		20 **E**		1		1
23	20	3	20	2		1	13	13	2	20 **E**	9	9	1	2
5		4		15		22				11 **L**		20		18
15	2	20	15	4	20		7	18	26	20 **E**	9	25	5	15
		2								16 **Y**		25		5
13	11	20	18	10							21	20	2	1
20														6
2	5	9	20					8	2	1	9	9
13		17		9						2
11	1	6	10	23	20	9	9		5	8	23	5	25	20
20		18		5			14		6		8			18
24	16	11	1	13	4	1	23	20		18	10	18	13	25
20		5		20		6		20		12		7		20
10	6	10	2	20	25	18	11	5		18	25	5	1	23

A B C D E F G H I J K L M N O P Q R S T U V W X Y Z

1	2	3	4	5	6	7	8	9	10	11 **L**	12	13
14	15	16 **Y**	17	18	19 **K**	20 **E**	21	22	23	24	25	26

Turn To P171-173 For Solutions

20 **E**	7	7	18	22	6	23	25	1	23

Choppy Waters

Can Bex help her husband overcome his fear, or must he face it alone?

By Tess Niland Kimber

Bex carried the newly unpacked wetsuits into the shop while Chris served the man at the till.

"And I'll need some anti-fog spray for the diving mask," the customer said.

She hung the wetsuits on the rail as Chris asked, "Will you be paying with cash or card?"

"Card, please… Oh and do you run any scuba diving courses?"

Bex looked up, her dark eyes watching her husband who was standing statue-like at the till. She held her breath, willing him

"But it's not good enough. We can't keep turning away lucrative business"

to answer but then she heard him say,

"Um…no, sir, sorry. Not any more."

"You sure? I was certain someone said DiveThru ran some great courses."

Chris looked uncomfortable, so Bex rescued him by saying, "Like my husband said, we don't run the courses any more."

Chris glanced at her, his relief palpable.

"That's a pity. Do you know anyone local who might?"

As Bex helped the man, giving him the contact details of their friend Amir, Chris moved away from the till. As he passed

her to go out to the back of the shop, she noticed his hands were shaking.

The customer left, jangling the bell over the door. Almost immediately Chris re-appeared, carrying two mugs of tea.

"We can't go on like this. I mean, I can't," he sighed.

"It's fine, Chris. We'll manage. We are managing." She smiled encouragingly.

"But it's not good enough. We can't keep turning away business. The courses – they used to be lucrative."

His dark eyes looked troubled as he

put her *Best Mum* mug on the counter.

Bex tucked her hand into his arm.

"It's only for now. The shop's doing all right. And those wetsuits will fly off the peg. When… you're back on your feet, we'll start the courses again."

Chris raised an eyebrow but didn't argue.

"Anyway, we've St Abbs to look forward to this weekend," she smiled.

"St Abbs – where it all started," he sighed, sipping his tea.

"You still want to go?"

"No… but I have to."

The boys were tired by the time they arrived at St Abbs, but the thought of a weekend with Granny Lucy soon perked them up.

Bex sighed, feeling the worries of the last few months ebb away as they drove into the village. That was the beauty of St Abbs. It was almost magical.

The harbour was as she remembered, ringed by rugged cliffs and with fishing boats moored in a line. The jetty curled out into the sea and gulls swooped overhead. Dog walkers and lovers wandered past the scattered fishermen's cottages.

She'd always loved her visits to St Abbs, except perhaps the last time…

"How about fish and chips for tea, boys?" Chris suggested.

Tiredness forgotten, their nine-year-old son Samuel and his seven-year-old brother Rowan jumped up and down on the quayside. "Yay!" ➡

Bex smiled. Maybe the trip away would be good for them. Good for Chris. But she felt uneasy. She shivered even in the warm July air, their last visit still etched on her mind…

Y ou're more mermaid than human," Chris laughed, as the dive boat O-Fish-Al took them out to sea.

"You can talk! Mum always said you had fins for arms."

Smiling, he'd winked at her, the weak February sun shining into his brown eyes.

"What are you hoping to see t'day?" Alistair asked as he steered.

Alistair Hadden was their captain of choice whenever they wanted to buddy dive. His safety procedures were second to none.

"A dolphin! I've never seen one," Bex said, already shivering in the chill sea air.

In St Abbs the cooler weather usually meant a shorter dive, but the sea was so crystal clear it made spotting the marine life they loved, much easier.

"Well, you might be lucky. The last group I took oot saw a pod."

"And I love the reef," Chris said, spraying his mask in readiness for the descent into the cold North Sea.

"Will the weather hold, Alistair?" she asked. It was the one factor that ruled her dives – that, and ensuring she'd enough oxygen in her tank.

"Aye, it should. There's a wee gale forecast but not 'til the morrow."

So, the dive that day started well. With a splash they slipped into the water from the moving platform at the stern and soon descended sixty feet. Here, the sea was like another planet, teeming with fish. Bex shone her torch and saw anemones, dead man's fingers and shoals of wolffish. It was beautiful. But where was her dolphin?

Chris swam to inspect the reef, giving her the thumbs up. And then she saw it. A beautiful grey shape undulating through the water. Her first dolphin! In awe, she watched as it swam close enough to touch. But as she turned to share the moment with Chris, she was horrified. He was flailing in the water. From his arm movements, this was an emergency! She shone her torch, immediately understanding. He'd got his foot trapped in the reef.

Quickly, she swam over and began to disentangle him but then she saw something she'd never expected with Chris on a buddy dive. His eyes wide, he was panicking. As soon as she pulled his foot from the reef, he started to ascend.

Slow down, she thought, knowing that breaking the surface too quickly can be dangerous. She followed, swimming faster than she'd like and feeling a little dizzy.

Seizing his hand, she forced him to pause at the safety stop. Any quicker and he'd get the bends for sure. She willed him to wait. Decompression sickness was a real danger to divers who rise too quickly. Chris knew this but in his panicked state, she was scared he'd try to break the waterline too early.

Finally, it was time to finish the ascent, and they bobbed above the surface, waiting for Alistair to pick them up. Bex was worried. Chris's teeth were chattering and there was a wild look in his dark eyes.

They clambered onto the lift and were soon aboard. Alistair took one look at Chris and wrapped him in a silver thermal blanket. Then without a word he set off for the shore. They left their diving gear with Alistair who promised, "I'll drop it all off later at Granny Lucy's."

Once back on dry land, Bex helped Chris into the van. "I'm taking you to the infirmary for a check-up," she insisted.

She expected him to argue but he just sat in the passenger seat, staring ahead.

The doctors at the hospital thankfully confirmed Chris was fine, just distressed.

But back in the van as Bex prepared to drive back to Granny Lucy's and the boys, Chris shocked her by saying, "I don't want to dive again. Not ever."

And he hadn't. Bex respected his decision, but it made life at DiveThru difficult. The courses which Chris had run at the local swimming pool and offshore ceased. Even managing the shop was a constant reminder to him of that day.

What had once united them – a love of diving – now divided them. Bex still loved the sport, but she could tell from his tense body language that Chris hated any mention of diving – even coming from their customers.

A few weeks later they were locking the front door of DiveThru at six-thirty when Chris suddenly whispered to her, "I could've drowned."

She reached for him, holding him close.

might be wise. It's hard, working in the shop with you."

"Really?"

"Yes, I can tell every inquiry, every sale, reminds you of that day. You need to make peace with diving or else we may have to think about selling the business."

He looked horrified.

"Surely it won't come to that?"

"I hope not but I hate you suffering."

Bex didn't want to push it, but she was pleased when a few days later Chris made an appointment with the doctor and then started some talking sessions with the mental health team.

That weekend, Bex, Chris and the boys went bowling. "Is the therapy helping?" she asked as they watched Samuel roll the bowling ball along the alley.

"I think so. It'll take time though."

"I'm proud of you. For seeking help," she smiled before taking her turn, groaning when her ball slipped off the runway into the gully.

The boys laughed and after Chris had bowled, he said, "I want us to go away."

"Can we afford a holiday?"

"I want to lose the fear. Diving brought me a lot of joy. I want to find it again"

When they pulled apart, she rested her hands on his shoulders,

"Yes, you could, but you didn't. Every diver experiences some difficulties, especially if they dive as much as we have. But the important thing is to end the dive safely, which you did. It'll be different next time."

"There won't be a next time. I never want to feel that fear again."

"Have you thought about… getting help? Talking to someone."

He frowned. "Do I need to?"

She took a deep breath. "I think it

"Not a proper one. But I'm thinking of going to St Abbs."

"To Granny Lucy's?"

"Yes – but also to do as you suggest."

"Me?" she frowned.

"You said I need to make peace with diving. Nowhere better than where all this happened."

"Do you feel ready?"

He watched Rowan use the ramp to help him bowl.

"I'm not, but I want to lose the fear. Diving brought me a lot of joy. I want to find that again." ➤

"St Abbs it is, then. Next weekend?"

"If Amir can work in the shop and Granny Lucy can have us."

Granny Lucy was delighted to open her home to Bex and her family.

"Lovely to see you all," she smiled, as she welcomed them into her cottage.

Granny Lucy was an artist who sold paintings of the yachts and fishing boats that visited the harbour.

Both Bex and Chris had lost their mothers before the boys were born but Granny Lucy had been her mum's best friend.

She'd happily taken on the role of surrogate grandmother and the boys adored her, as did Chris and Bex.

"All OK?" she asked after the boys had gone upstairs with Chris to unpack.

Bex put the kettle on the stove as Granny Lucy reached down and opened a battered tin of home-made shortbread.

"Well, after our last visit Chris hasn't

That evening they all enjoyed a noisy time round Granny Lucy's kitchen table, eating fish and chips from the paper and then playing a game of Hasty Patience, with Rowan winning almost every round, much to Samuel's disgust.

"Can't win everything, Sam," Granny Lucy hugged him. "You won Monopoly last time you stayed."

Reminded of his past brilliance, Samuel was happier by the time the boys went to bed.

"So, what plans do you have for the 'morrow?" Granny Lucy asked.

"If you don't mind looking after the boys, we're going out…" Chris said, quietly. "With Alistair. In O-Fish-Al."

Now it was Bex's turn to be anxious as the small boat rode the waves. Chris was in his diving gear, the first time he'd worn his wetsuit since that February day.

"Are you sure you're OK to do this?"

"Let's not do this. It's enough that you've come out in the boat today"

been himself. That last dive really scared him. He's not been back in the water since," she confided in a whisper.

Granny Lucy looked suitably shocked.

"I canna imagine Chris not in the water. Don't worry – he'll come round."

Bex shrugged. "I'm not so sure. He's having therapy but life's hard in the shop. Everything reminds him of that day. He can't help giving off negative vibes to our customers. I'm thinking… we may have to shut DiveThru."

"Oh no! You canna let that happen."

Bex broke a biscuit in half, trying to be good as she had fish and chips to look forward to later, and said, "He asked to come back to St Abbs. I'm hoping it'll be cathartic. If not, who knows?"

she asked him for the hundredth time.

"No, but every diver feels some fear before they dive."

Bex nodded. "But a diver needs to be calm. To regulate their breathing. You don't have to do this."

As Alistair found the right spot, Bex prepared to climb onto the dive lift. Chris sat next to her, but she could see he wasn't ready. "Let's not do this. It's enough you've come out today."

"You think so?"

"Definitely."

Back in the harbour, Granny Lucy was painting outdoors while the boys kicked a football to each other. Bex and Chris joined them.

"We decided we want to go diving, Daddy," Samuel said.

"Well, you're a little young yet…"

Bex looked at her family and then had a sudden brainwave. "They are – but I've got an idea."

After a trip to the shop, they were all soon kitted out. Granny Lucy stayed at the water's edge with her easel while the family of four went into the clear water.

"OK?" Bex asked Chris.

He nodded and then with both boys in tow, he slipped on the snorkelling mask. "This is what you need to learn first," he told the boys, showing them how to control their breathing.

"Is it dangerous?" Rowan asked.

"Not if we do everything as we should. And we don't need to go under the water – we can look through our masks at the water creatures just below the surface."

They found a small pool not far from the water's edge and Chris told the boys how to look under the water and swim wearing their fins.

"Can you show me, Daddy?"

Bex glanced at Chris who had suddenly stilled. He looked back at her and she nodded.

"Yes… yes, I think I can."

He took a few deep breaths, slipped on his mask, and then slowly put his face down into the water.

Bex held her own breath as Chris began swimming in the shallow pool, thrilled that he was starting to lose the fear that had gripped him for so long.

Moments later, Samuel emulated his father. Then Rowan and Bex dipped their heads into the sea.

"This is so cool! I saw a shark and a whale and a seal and everything!" Samuel told his younger brother.

"A shark? Did you really?" Bex laughed.

"Well, I think it was," he said, glancing away from her.

I loved that!" Chris exclaimed as they all walked back to Granny Lucy's whitewashed cottage.

Bex hugged him close.

"I'm so pleased. Do you think it's helped? That you might go diving again one day?"

He fell silent for a moment and then remarked, "I think I've learned something today."

"And?" she smiled.

"That the water isn't about scuba or deep-sea diving or even snorkelling. It's about having fun. And if I'm happy, what does it matter if I never dive again?"

"True. It's also about being safe and feeling safe. You can't enjoy a sport if you don't feel that." They followed the boys and Granny Lucy past the bistro.

"And it's also about my knowledge. Years of diving experience can't be wiped away, even if I never feel able to scuba dive again. I still have something to give to the customers."

"Of course you do," Bex said. She thought for a moment and then added, "I think I understand. Snorkelling with the boys showed you can still have fun and pass on your knowledge, even if you aren't scuba diving. Do you think you might feel happier in the shop again?"

"I'm sure I will… I'm not saying I'll never dive again. I hope I will. But if I don't, I've the shop and you, the boys…"

"And we can all go snorkelling again, can't we, Dad?" Samuel said, looking back over his shoulder.

"You bet!" Chris laughed.

And as they walked up the hill to Granny Lucy's cottage in the late afternoon sun, Bex smiled. It seemed St Abbs had worked its magic once more. ⓜ

Tortilla Pizza Pies

Ingredients (Makes 8)

- ◆ **2 large soft flour tortillas**
- ◆ **100g pizza sauce**
- ◆ **100g frozen peppers, defrosted and chopped**
- ◆ **50g pepperoni, chopped**
- ◆ **50g mature Cheddar cheese, grated**
- ◆ **1 large egg, beaten**
- ◆ **100ml whole milk**
- ◆ **40g pitted black olives, sliced**

1 Preheat the oven to 180°C, Fan Oven 160°C, Gas Mark 4. Grease 8 cupcake tins. Cut out 4 x 10cm circles from each tortilla using a cookie cutter, and carefully fold and press into the tins to form cases.

2 Mix the pizza sauce, peppers and pepperoni together and spoon into the cases. Sprinkle over the cheese. Mix the egg and milk and pour on top. Sprinkle with olives.

3 Bake for about 25min until set. Cool for 15min to firm up before loosening with a knife to remove from the tins. Cool on a wire rack. Chill before packing and serve with fresh basil, olives and salad.

RECIPES AND STYLING KATHRYN HAWKINS PHOTOGRAPHY STUART MACGREGOR

Just Us

Ten days in the romantic spot where they'd spent their honeymoon – would their marriage survive it?

By Gillian Harvey

The holiday hadn't been their idea. "Well, thirty years together ought to be celebrated," Tish had said, handing them an envelope.

Inside, they'd found tickets for an all expenses paid trip to Nice.

"A second honeymoon!" their daughter had beamed triumphantly.

"Wow, Nice," Clare had said as she'd opened the envelope. "Look, love. She's bought us a trip to Nice."

"Wow," he'd said, taking the tickets. "You really shouldn't have."

"Don't be daft," Tish had said. "I wanted to. You guys never take a break."

They'd made all the right noises, but Clare suspected she and Gary had similar feelings about the trip. Yes, they had been married for thirty years; and yes, they were still relatively happy. But

they weren't in that place anymore. Sure, they spent the odd weekend together in Norfolk from time to time, but for the most part, he went on golfing trips with his club, and she did the odd spa retreat with the girls.

After thirty years of marriage, the thought of 10 days of enforced proximity wasn't as appealing as it might once had been. They hadn't been on holiday together properly for almost a decade.

Tish was newly married – and Clare could hardly tell her loved-up thirty-year-old that while marriages might 'work' – in that couples stayed together – they weren't always as wonderful as they might seem from the outside. There was a togetherness, sure. But not the spark there had once been.

Still, she loved Gary and they'd make the best of it. They had to – it was a gift.

"If Ben and I are half as happy as you

two in thirty years' time," Tish had said, raising her glass, "then I'll count myself the luckiest woman on Earth," and she'd smiled at her husband, who'd returned her gaze, his eyes swimming with affection.

Clare had looked at Gary, who'd looked back and raised an eyebrow. Poor kids had no idea of what marriage your relationship to each other. Romantic spontaneity gave way to practical planning. Gestures of love came in the form of cups of tea in bed rather than roses, chocolates or meals in a fancy restaurant.

And those practicalities sort of shifted what you were to each other. Not making

Gestures of love now came in the form of cups of tea in bed rather than roses

really meant, not really. They hadn't yet endured hardships together, raised children together. They hadn't faced financial problems, redundancy, illness, or the kind of happy stresses that crop up over the years – new jobs, new houses, new horizons.

Those experiences changed you. Brought you closer, but also changed things worse; just making them different.

She loved Gary, of course she did. And he loved her too. It was just they'd settled into a different phase of love, she supposed. The kind of love that was dependable, that meant you always had someone by your side if you needed to go to the hospital, or that one of them would always prepare dinner for the other; ➔

where you didn't always bother to spruce yourself up if you weren't going anywhere. The kind of familial love that came with years of ups and downs, rather than the romantic love couples had at the start.

And that was fine with her. And him. They were content.

She couldn't help but worry, though, as she stuffed shorts and T-shirts into their shared suitcase a few weeks later, that being forced to spend time together in a romantic location; the very place they'd spent their honeymoon, in fact, would simply expose the cracks that had formed in their relationship over the years.

Rather than connect them, she worried walking the streets they'd strolled hand-in-hand thirty years ago would make them both realise what they'd lost – how far they were from that happy couple with their hopes, dreams and passions.

Would being together for ten uninterrupted days force them to confront the fact that they weren't really *in love* any more? Would it take them from a place where they were satisfied to a yearning for more?

Of course, the fact that they weren't in the first flush of love wouldn't be news to either of them, she thought, clicking the case shut then opening a bag to fill with toiletries, plus their various medications which – Gary had joked – might need a passport all of their own. They both knew how things were between them – that they snuggled up on the sofa, but rarely held hands. They slept in the same bed, but rarely – if ever – made love.

It was fine when they were living their lives in their three-bed semi in Welwyn. Their daily activities were moulded together like jigsaw pieces. They had their roles within the relationship, and stuck to them faithfully.

But having to juxtapose their settled contentment against a romantic backdrop? Well, Clare couldn't help but worry whether it might somehow break them. Shatter their simple, companionable contentment and make them start to wonder whether it was really enough.

She zipped up the now-rattling bag then made her way down to the living room where Gary was watching the start of the motor racing.

"Just a sec," he said, holding up a finger as she entered the room. A minute later, the finger lowered. "Go on," he said. "Sorry – don't want to …"

"…miss the start," she said. "I know, don't worry. Just wanted to say that I've done the packing, but you might want to check through your stuff to make sure…"

"Oh, you didn't have to do that!" he said. It was a reflex more than anything. She always did the packing.

In Gary's defence, he kept the garden tidy and neat, and wasn't afraid to roll up his sleeves and wash up each evening after dinner. Over the years they'd settled into their roles, each taking a share of the chores until each of them had their official tasks to do around the house.

It was an even split, and she didn't mind packing – although it had been a long time since she'd had to pack for anything over a few days away.

"Are you looking forward to it?" she asked him later, tucking a strand of blonde hair behind her ear as they settled in front of the news with a glass of red wine.

"Of course," he said, taking a sip. "Always loved France in the summer."

She nodded. "Yes, me too," she said. "It's just that…"

He looked at her quizzically.

"What's up?"

But she didn't know how to put her feeling into words.

"Not sure," she said. "I just feel like I've forgotten something, I suppose."

"Don't worry, I'll check through everything later," he said, patting her knee as the opening credits began.

She looked at him as the programme – a TV drama about divorce lawyers who seemed incapable of keeping a relationship together – flickered light onto his face. Did he feel the same about the trip? Or was he genuinely looking forward to it? It was hard to tell; impossible to ask.

She'd just have to get on with it, she supposed. Make the best of it and hope things would turn out OK.

It had been three years since she'd been on a plane, but the next morning she found that being in the airport felt just as it always did: the strange mixture of exciting, boring and stressful that came

throw them, as a couple, into sharp relief. Might force them to realise that although their relationship was good, it wasn't what it had once been.

Still, she managed to relax as the plane taxied and bumped along the runway, faster and faster until it lurched into the air, rapidly gaining height. She felt the ground falling away and with it all the everyday stress of life. The shopping, cleaning, part-time work as a solicitor – all of it – became small and insignificant. She'd forgotten what it had meant to properly 'get away', she realised. To actually shed the life you lived each day, like a snake wriggling from its skin, and feel somehow released.

She glanced at Gary, and he glanced back. "It's been too long," he said.

"Yes," she agreed. "Far too long."

Clare watched as patchwork fields gave way to sea, which turned from grey to blue as they crossed the Channel, then passed tiny cliffs, postage-stamp beaches, fields with tiny towns dotted about haphazardly between.

She felt the distance stretching behind them – the miles clocking up between her and Clare the mum, Clare the daughter, Clare the part-time lawyer, Clare the person who could always be relied on to

All the roles she'd adopted over the years had each come with a little weight

with jumping through security hoops, finding gates, browsing books and finally being called to board.

As she fastened her seatbelt in a seat next to his, he touched her hand briefly and gave it a squeeze.

"Here's to thirty years," he said.

She smiled. "Yes. And they've been good ones," she said, still feeling a frisson of nerves that somehow forcing themselves on a romantic retreat might

pick something up from the shop on her way home.

She felt as if she'd removed a heavy backpack from her shoulders. Not because she didn't like being all of those things, but because those roles that she'd adopted automatically over the years had each come with a little weight; a little responsibility; expectations of others. And it was nice, just for a bit, to feel that those parts of her could be rested and ➡

let go, just for a little while. What was left? Simply Clare. Or – she glanced at Gary – Clare the wife. She reached over and put her hand on Gary's. He looked at her then turned his palm upwards and held her hand properly.

"Not long now," he said.

Exiting the airport was the usual combination of stressful and patience-testing, but when they emerged through the glass doors onto the sun-drenched concourse, they were able to slide into a taxi straight away.

Within minutes they were on a dual carriageway, which gave way to a smaller road, edged with neat beige buildings, then down another until they emerged onto a road adjacent to the azure sea.

Then the taxi finally pulled up at their destination, Royal Riviera.

When Clare and Gary had first come to France, full of excitement and hope and all the things that come with being twenty-four and newly married, their accommodation had been modest – a small chambre d'hôte half a mile from the front, where they'd been overwhelmed with the kindness of their host, and thrilled at the tiny balcony in front of their room.

But neither of them had gasped.

luxurious, it had a quirky layout – with a wooden reception desk, old fashioned wood panelling and the sort of lights normally seen above pool tables. It was sleek, but somehow homely at once.

"Parlez-vous anglais?" Gary said inexpertly to the young man at the reception desk. "J'ai un… um, booking pour un room? Pour moi and my wife?"

"Of course, we all speak English here," the man replied in perfect English, which somehow sounded even better with his French accent than it did when either of them spoke. "It is a pleasure to welcome you to Royal Riviera. Let me show you to your room." Gary caught Clare's eye and she had to hold back a giggle at both his attempt at French and the fact that it had been completely unnecessary.

After marvelling again at the room their daughter had splashed out on, they unpacked then, changing into more appropriate clothing for the 30-degree heat – shorts and a chequered shirt for him, a green, knee-length dress for her – made their way down to the bar area and the terrace that overlooked the ocean.

"Well, cheers to us," said Gary at last when he wobbled back to the table with two beers on a tray. He held out his

"You know, if I'm honest, I wasn't really looking forward to this holiday"

This time, both of them did, as they stared up at the hotel their daughter had booked for them.

"It's right on the seafront," said Gary. "It's practically in the water."

"And it's so… well, posh," said Clare. "How can Tish have afforded this? It must have cost her a fortune!"

They paid the driver, and, picking up their luggage, made their way into the marbled foyer. Although the hotel was

glass and she clinked it. Then they both sipped, looking out over the palm trees and hearing the gentle swoosh of waves against rock just metres away.

"Thirty years, eh?"

"Thirty years," she said, looking at him.

"You know," he said, thoughtfully, putting his beer down. "If I'm honest, I wasn't looking forward to this holiday."

"No?" she said, trying to act surprised.

"Yeah," he said, rubbing a hand

through his silver peppered hair. "No offence or anything. It's just been a while since it… since we…"

"Since it was just us?" she suggested gently.

"Yeah," he said. "It sounds stupid, probably. Because it's only us at home now. So we're often… well, alone together. But it's all the things… you know. Work and that. Tish. Getting her settled. The house stuff… and look, I know I don't always pull my weight but…"

"You do OK," she said, more interested in where the conversation was going than entering the familiar cul-de-sac of who did what around the house.

"Anyway, now we're here I kind of feel different. A bit more like myself again."

"I know exactly what you mean," she answered softly.

"And it's weird, but it suddenly doesn't seem long, does it, since we were last here?" he said.

"Hardly any time at all," she smiled. "And at the same time, it feels as if it was a hundred years ago."

He nodded. "Weird isn't it," he said, sipping again from his glass. "Anyway, I wanted to say… I was kind of nervous about coming here together. You know? But now we're here, I just feel more… well, different about it."

"Excited?" she suggested.

"Yeah, that," he said. "I mean, I feel like we've sort of time travelled. Like you're Clare and I'm Gaz and we're here for the first time."

"Only in a far posher hotel," she said.

"Definitely," he grinned. "Much posher." Then, "Do you remember that woman… you know, the one at the restaurant?" he said. "Yes!" Clare laughed. "She practically threw our food at us when we asked for our steaks well done."

"And that guy at the hotel, who kept talking to me in the bar for, what – a century?"

"Oh yes. I was asleep in our room by the time you got away."

"Not for long though," he said, raising an eyebrow.

"No," she said, finding to her surprise that her cheeks had flushed at the memory. She sipped her beer and looked over the view.

"Not for long."

"Anyway – here's to us. To relaxing, and having a bit of fun."

"And to it being 'just us,'" she said.

"Yes. To just us."

They clinked their glasses, then he drained the last of his.

"Another?" he asked.

"Why not."

As she sat on the terrace, feeling the sun on her face for the first time in months, and hearing the clink of bottles being opened in the nearby bar, Clare found she was smiling.

Not because everything in their relationship had suddenly been repaired by their being away. Not because she was already feeling a little giddy from the beer and bubbles.

But because she'd discovered that with all the barriers removed – all the minutiae of day-to-day life: the trials, tribulations, responsibility and stress –they were just Clare and Gary again.

She hadn't found an absence of feeling at all; just a long-forgotten, overlooked connection. And ten days in the sun to explore and celebrate that once again.

Missing Link

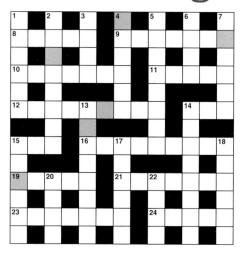

The answer to each clue is a word which has a link with each of the three words listed. This word may come at the end (eg **HEAD** linked with **BEACH, BIG, HAMMER**), at the beginning (eg **BLACK** linked with **BEAUTY, BOARD and JACK**) or a mixture of the two (eg **STONE** linked with **HAIL, LIME and WALL**).

ACROSS

8 Footing, Pay, Rights (5)
9 Patients, Specimens, Students (7)
10 Country, Hasty, Religious (7)
11 Clerical, Computer, Message (5)
12 Blank, Ink, Paper (9)
14 Electric, Grass, Jellied (3)
15 Stream, Summer, Wife (3)
16 Planning, Points, Weapons (9)
19 Fibre, Philosophy, Victory (5)
21 Bank, Beam, Sheet (7)
23 Account, Medical, Sheet (7)
24 Board, Piece, Set (5)

DOWN

1 Measure, System, Weight (6)
2 Pearls, Person, Probiotics (8)
3 Or, Something, Where (4)
4 Argument, Centrally, Over (6)
5 Artist, Cafe, Moving (8)
6 Brighton, Glass, Wigan (4)
7 Pump, Tank, Unleaded (6)
13 Cattle, Leaves, Skirts (8)
14 Civil, Electrical, Mechanical (8)
15 Life, Private, State (6)
17 Armed, Bank, Grave (6)
18 Big, Cloth, Macaroni (6)
20 Ladder, Skipping, Tow (4)
22 Combination, Jaw, Pad (4)

Hidden word in the shaded squares: _____

Sudoku

7		6		1				
	9		7					
		5		6		9		7
	2		3	7	4			9
3			1	9	8		6	
8		1		5		3		
					1		2	
				3		7		4

Fill in each of the blank squares with the numbers 1 to 9, so that each row, each column and each 3x3 cell contains all the numbers from 1 to 9.

Word Wheel

Turn To P171-173 For Solutions

You have ten minutes to find as many words as possible using the letters in the wheel. Each word must be three letters or more and contain the central letter. Use each letter once and no plurals, foreign words or proper nouns are allowed. There is at least one nine-letter word.

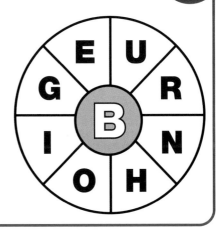

Average: 30 words
Good: 31-45 words
Excellent: 46-59 words

Say It With Flowers

A beautiful bouquet of red roses managed to start
an entire conversation all by themselves!

By Ginny Swart

Ellen Wilson stared at the woman from
the florist's shop on her doorstep.
She could barely see her face behind the
enormous bouquet of red roses. "For me?
But who'd send me flowers?"

"I don't know, but I'm sure the note
will tell you," smiled the girl. "You know
what red roses mean, don't you? Must be
from someone who loves you a lot!"

Ellen couldn't think of a single soul
who loved her enough to spend a fortune
on an armful of long-stemmed red roses.
She closed the door slowly and studied
the handwriting before she opened the
envelope: *Can't help thinking of you all
day.* Unsigned. Who was this anonymous
person who was thinking of her? And
why? It wasn't her birthday.

Not likely. Her daughter Jane? Impossible.
She was hiking somewhere in Thailand.

Then she had sudden wild, ridiculous
thought. Could it be Mr Hammerton
from the library? She noticed lately how
he asked her opinion on what she'd read
when she changed her books. How he
watched her making her selection and
the comments he made when he stamped
them out. And only last week, she'd
taken out *The Victorian Dictionary of the
Language of Flowers*!

Mr Hammerton had smiled and said,
"I believe that in the past, people used
flowers to say what they were too shy to
put into words. I'm sure you'll enjoy this."

She reached for the book, still unread,
with its beautiful flower illustrations, and
ran her finger down the list of names.
"Roses… roses.. ah, Roses, red: True

People used to use flowers to say what they were too shy to put into words

She took them through to the kitchen
of her flat and ran the sink full of water for
them. The roses made a blaze of colour
in her tiny kitchen, which badly needed
a coat of paint. Ellen made herself a
cup of tea and sat down, going over the
possibilities in her mind.

Her son Alan? With three little ones
under the age of five and a big mortgage?

Love! Well I never. Mr Hammerton!"

Humming to herself, she arranged the
lovely blooms in a vase. Then she curled
up on the sofa with the book and read it
from start to finish with deep interest.

Next morning she was on her way to
the library when she ran into Mischa
returning to the apartment next door.

"Lovely morning, isn't it?" she beamed.

"Is it? It's pouring rain," said Mischa, who looked as if she'd been crying.

"I love rain," said Ellen, "Invigorating." Mischa sniffed and went inside.

Young people sometimes looked so stressed, thought Ellen. The poor girl needs a holiday.

She couldn't help smiling when she saw Mr Hammerton in his usual spot behind the counter of the library.

"Good morning, Miss Wilson. Er…

raining out today, is it?" he asked.

Ellen smiled gaily. "A bit damp, that's all. Lovely weather for flowers."

"Ah yes, Enjoyed this one, did you?" Mr Hammerton looked at *The Language of Flowers* on top of her pile.

"Yes, very much, very informative. And as you said, a wonderful way for shy people to say what they want to."

He nodded absent-mindedly and put her books onto the trolley behind him.

"Oh, Mr Hammerton, I nearly ➔

forgot!" Ellen dived into her basket and produced a pot plant, which she put on the counter. "A cyclamen," she said distinctly. "I thought it might cheer up your desk."

"Why, Miss Wilson. That's most kind. What a nice thought. Thank you."

"It's a cyclamen," she repeated meaningfully. "And do call me Ellen, please." If Mr Hammerton was anything like most men, he wouldn't know a daisy from a dandelion. "Well, I'd better start choosing my books I suppose. Can't stand here chatting all morning."

She selected a thriller, which she didn't remember reading before, then thought of something and hurried back to the desk.

"How many copies does the library

Ellen was not disappointed.

On the counter next to her cyclamen plant stood a vase containing a solitary purple iris. She knew this meant something but couldn't remember what.

"My, what a beautiful bloom, Mr Hammerton," she said. "I didn't know you were a gardener?"

"I do my best," he said. "I have a great affection for these, but the moles got the rest of them. Lovely colour, isn't it?"

She renewed her copy of *The Language of Flowers* and as fast as was decent, she hastened through the library to the seclusion of the furthest stacks, and feverishly thumbed through the pages… *Iris: Deep and Warm Affection.*

Oh my goodness! And how subtle

He casually used her name for the first time, as though he'd always done so

have of that flower dictionary?" she asked.

"Ah, let me see…" Mr Hammerton punched the keyboard and peered short-sightedly at the screen. "Three."

"Oh, well, in that case I'd like to take it out again, if I may," she said. "Fascinating book. Have you read it?"

"I've, er… dipped into it," he said. Was he blushing? Ellen couldn't tell.

She could hardly wait to return to the library to see if he had an answer for her. She'd chosen a pot of cyclamen because it meant *Modesty* and *Shyness*, which she felt was the correct response for Mr Hammerton, who apart from this single mad impulsive gesture seemed to be an old-fashioned man. She couldn't really expect him to send another bouquet on his librarian's salary, although he'd certainly made his intentions clear. She was sure he'd find some more economical way to communicate with her.

he'd been in re-enforcing his message! She flushed with happiness and floated between the shelves, hardly aware of which books she was choosing.

As she waited for him to stamp them out, Ellen noticed he was wearing a new name badge: Michael Hammerton.

"There you are, Ellen," he said, casually using her name for the first time, as though he'd always done so.

"Thank you, Michael," she answered as lightly as she could, and gave him her best smile. "See you soon."

He watched her walk away and she waved her fingers at him as she left.

What should her response be? She turned the pages anxiously to find the right flower. *Deep and warm affection…* she was tempted to reply with Red Valerian meaning *Readiness*, but she didn't know what Red Valerian looked like and besides, she didn't want to appear too keen. Man was supposed to be the

hunter, after all. Dragon Wort meant *Astonishment*, but she'd got over her initial surprise. Perhaps it was time to move on to something more positive… but not too expensive – the cyclamen had cost rather a lot.

In the end she settled for plain old straw, which indicated *Agreement*. Well, she agreed with affection. Not as exciting as true love but more lasting, somehow. It had a comforting ring to it.

She'd found a handful of dried grass which could pass for straw and pinned it to her cardigan, backing it up with a saucy little straw hat left over from summer. She had to put the hood of her raincoat over it to stop it dissolving in the rain on the way to the library, and arrived feeling a little flustered.

"I do like your hat, if you don't mind my saying so," said Michael. "Brings a bit of cheer to a dark day. What are those? Candytuft?"

"What? Oh!" Too late she realised there were some tatty old silk flowers on the brim. Candytuft. *Indifference.* Oh heavens, wrong, wrong, wrong! She snatched the hat off her head and held it out. "I've always liked a straw hat," she said. "Reminds me of the beach. Picnics, that sort of thing. My favourite season is summer!"

"I couldn't agree with you more," he said gravely.

He was certainly quick on the uptake. He must have been poring over the book as well.

Then her eye fell on his buttonhole. A rosebud. Sort of orange coloured.

"Nice rosebud," she smiled encouragingly.

"Yes, Coral Beauty. I thought I'd try my hand at roses this year."

She flushed crimson and said in a shaking voice, "Well that is a beauty."

Coral roses: *Desire!* Really, Michael was almost too forward!

Well, she had the answer to that one! No point in waiting around at our age, she thought, I'll buy a jonquil. Maybe wear it in my hair next time. *Affection returned.*

At what point, she wondered, is he actually planning to say something?

Back in her flat Ellen was making herself a cup of tea and admiring her gorgeous roses which had become full blown rosettes of deep red. She'd put them on the coffee table where they filled the whole room with their heady perfume and she was just wondering if she should try and press one as a keepsake, when there was knock on the door.

It was Mischa, looking a bit discomfited.

"Miss Wilson, I think you might have had my flowers," she blurted. "My boyfriend says he sent me a bunch after we had a fight last week but I never received them."

"Your flowers? Were they red roses?"

"Yes. My boyfriend phoned the florist and they said they'd delivered them to Number 10. That's you. I'm number 11."

Ellen swallowed. "Yes, I have them," she croaked. "But they didn't have a name on them, so I thought…"

"Not to worry!" said Mischa cheerfully. "We made up the next day anyway. He just thought it was weird that I didn't thank him for his surprise."

Frozen-faced, Ellen wrapped the rather withered blooms in newspaper and ➤

gave them to their rightful owner. Then she shut the front door and allowed the tears to fall.

So the roses hadn't been from Michael Hammerton. So he hadn't followed up with a message of deep and warm affection, he'd just been rescuing his last remaining iris from the moles. So the coral-coloured rosebud was a co-incidence. And of course he wasn't planning to say something. Ever.

He probably hadn't even looked at the dictionary of flowers, and her cyclamen meant nothing to him, not did her straw. She didn't know whether to be relieved or sorry.

As you were, you foolish woman, as you were, she told herself.

She straightened her shoulders and made herself another cup of tea. And opened some chocolate biscuits.

Enjoy it?"

"Oh – yes. Well, quaint, really, isn't it?"

"Full of interest, I thought. I read it properly for the first time over the weekend."

"Oh, yes?" Her eyes were drawn to the bright buttonhole he was sporting in his tweed jacket.

"Yes. What an amazing book! I was hoping you'd be in today so we could exchange notes. I see you're admiring my pansy?"

"Yes," she whispered. "A yellow one. It's beautiful." *You occupy my thoughts.*

"I had no idea my garden was so eloquent! I have the most perfect damask

So the roses hadn't been from him after all – what a foolish woman she'd been!

In her haste during her last visit to the library, Ellen had taken out an odd assortment of books as well as renewing the dictionary of flowers. She was forced to plod through the third volume of a politician's memoirs, a book on bee keeping and an Inspector Morse she'd read twice before.

However, after a week she couldn't put off exchanging her books for something more readable.

Play it cool, Ellen, she thought. *A friendly smile is all that's required.*

"Good morning, Michael." There, calm as you please. But she couldn't help noticing the pretty bunch of sweet peas in a jam-jar on his counter. *A hoped-for meeting.*

"Good morning Ellen. Ah – returning the Victorian flower dictionary, are you?

roses out along the fence and my phlox are going to make a real show this year."

Bashful love and *Our hearts are united.*

"I haven't the luxury of a garden," she said. "But my pot plants console me."

"I'm sure that those can be very rewarding too."

"I have some very pretty jonquils just coming up in my window box."

They smiled at each other in perfect understanding.

"Ellen," he said, clearing his throat, "Could I invite you to tea on Saturday? To see my garden?"

"Thank you, Michael," she said. "That would be very nice."

I'll try and find some celandine seedlings to give him, she thought. *Joys to come.* Ⓜ

Brain Boosters

Missing Link

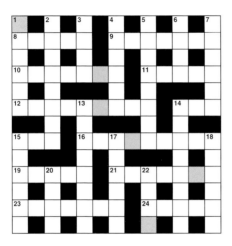

The answer to each clue is a word which has a link with each of the three words listed. This word may come at the end (eg **HEAD** linked with **BEACH, BIG, HAMMER**), at the beginning (eg **BLACK** linked with **BEAUTY, BOARD** and **JACK**) or a mixture of the two (eg **STONE** linked with **HAIL, LIME** and **WALL**).

ACROSS

8 Board, Cloth, Paper (5)
9 Jacket, Morocco, Patent (7)
10 Dramatics, Golf, Radio (7)
11 Ball, Chorus, Land (5)
12 City, Red, Square (9)
14 Dust, Pedal, Wheelie (3)
15 Gray's, Holiday, Keeper (3)
16 Arsenic, Food, Lead (9)
19 Dance, Rattling, Tooth (5)
21 Bird, Clock, Weight (7)
23 Kitchen, Natty, Welsh (7)
24 Be, Volumes, Wheel (5)

DOWN

1 Park, Price, Sector (6)
2 Distan, Poor, Ship (8)
3 Flat, Lever, Spare (4)
4 Broccoli, Cauliflower, Silk (6)
5 Boxing, Bush, Court (8)
6 Coal, Grill, Lady (4)
7 Cell, Open, Visitor (6)
13 Bar, Cup, Double (8)
14 Beach, Pavilion, Rock (8)
15 Job, Leg, Track (6)
17 Dive, Investment, Looking (6)
18 Belt, Snake, Stitch (6)
20 Pure, Thorough, Well (4)
22 Acid, Card, Drive (4)

Turn To P171-173 For Solutions

Hidden word in the shaded squares: _____

Saving The Caretta

Ella was off to university – but first, she had a far more important, world-changing task to undertake…

By Christina Collins

Ella had made her decision. Now she just needed to run it by her parents.

"So, I'm going to take a gap year."

"What do you mean, a gap year?" her dad enquired, as he folded his Sunday newspaper and placed it on the table.

Her mum turned from the sink, drying her hands on the tea towel.

"I feel I've done nothing but study for the past five years. I need a break, away from the books."

"But your place is all lined up at uni. We've spent months traipsing all over the country with you." Her dad frowned over the top of his tortoiseshell framed glasses.

"I won't give up my place, Dad. I still intend to go – I'll just defer for a year."

"You can do that?"

a plan." Ella opened her laptop and moved her fingers effortlessly across the keyboard before she turned the screen to face her parents. "I've signed up for this. I'm planning on leaving next week."

They read the page in front of them.

Volunteers are needed to help protect the endangered Loggerhead Turtle at Laganas Bay, Zante.

"So what will you be doing there?" her mum asked, seemingly intrigued now with Ella's idea.

"Laganas Bay is the largest breeding ground for the Caretta – the Loggerhead Turtle. They return every year to the beach where they were born to lay their eggs – but they hatch in the height of the tourist season when the beaches get crammed with holidaymakers.

"Out of every thousand or so

Out of every thousand hatchlings, only one will live to become an adult"

Her mum replied before she could.

"Ella, I know exactly what that means. A gap year is just another expression for *I don't want to go!*"

Ella sighed. "No. That's not going to happen, Mum."

"Well, you can't sit around doing nothing for a year," her dad warned.

"I don't intend to do nothing. I have

hatchlings, only one will make it to the sea and live to become an adult turtle."

Her mum lifted her hand to her mouth.

"Gosh, that's awful. What can the volunteers do to help them?"

"Make people aware really, patrolling the beach, watching the nests and stuff.

"The more people that are aware, the more hatchlings can attempt the journey

from the nesting ground to the sea."

"Well, Ella, I think that is an absolutely wonderful thing for you to do. And you're quite right – uni will still be there next year," her dad said proudly.

"Thanks, Dad." She wrapped her arms around him and hugged him tightly.

She looked up at her mum, who hesitated before nodding her approval.

A week later, Ella headed to the Greek island of Zante. There were no night flights into the island as the lights confused the newly hatched turtles heading for the sea.

She was met at the airport by Claire, one of the volunteers.

"Welcome to Zante," she said cheerily. "Let's get you settled into your digs. You're in the Rosa apartments in Kalamaki. They're small and basic, but it's

an easy walk from there to the seafront."

"Thanks, that sounds great."

"We've got a couple more volunteers arriving early afternoon so we've arranged a little get-together at Milo's Bar, it's just up the road from the Rosa. Give everyone a chance to meet each other."

"Will you be there?" Ella asked, suddenly feeling a little lost.

"Aye, I'll be there, but I know most of the regular volunteers, I've been volunteering for the last twelve years. Moved to the island four years ago, and never looked back."

Ella unpacked her bag and folded her clothes into the small chest of drawers. A double bed took up most of the space, and wooden doors led to a small balcony with just enough space for two chairs and a tiny round table, where the faint smell of citronella still lingered. ➔

There was no air conditioning, but the room did have its own bathroom.

She needed to take a shower before heading to Milo's. She squeezed her way past the washbasin and eyed the small spray nozzle hanging precariously on a hook poking out of the tiles. As she turned the tap, the showerhead promptly fell to the floor and spurted out cold water as bubbles surged back out of the tiny plastic drain cover. Despite its problems, Ella was grateful for the privacy.

She changed into a cool cotton dress with capped sleeves, slipped on her flip flops and made her way to Milo's Bar. It was a traditional taverna, with small wooden tables laid outside under a veranda that was adorned with bougainvillaea, its colourful bracts providing a vibrant pink display.

Ella hovered nervously outside; the bar was busy. Chatter and laughter spilled out onto the street.

"Ella, over here."

She turned to see Claire waving and made her way over.

"This is Luke, Paul and Abbie."

Waves and smiles were directed at her and she felt the warmth of their friendliness.

"The others will be here soon." Claire pulled out a chair. "And this is Lena, and George, they arrived today too. George has come from Australia!"

"Hi, it's lovely to meet you both."

George smiled, "You too. Now, what you drinking?"

"I'll have a small beer please."

George rose and strolled to the bar and she made polite conversation with Lena until he returned.

"So, Australia. A long way to come to do volunteering work."

His dark hair flopped over his face and he ran his fingers over his head, pushing the hair out of his eyes.

"It's a bit of a long story but I'm Greek Australian. My grandfather was born in Zante, not far from here, near Zante town. So it was a chance for me to see where I'm from, as well as doing my bit for the environment."

Ellas was intrigued.

"So, the Australian bit?"

George's lips curled, blue eyes highlighting his attractive features. His olive skin glowed with a thin layer of perspiration.

"That's the slushy part," he chuckled.

"Please continue."

"Well, my grandfather worked for his father on the boats and they sold most of their catch to local restaurants. One of the restaurants had recently hired a new waitress – my grandmother. Can you see where this is going?"

"I think I can, but tell me anyway."

"That's it really. They fell in love, but my grandmother got homesick so they both returned to Australia."

"So, do you still have family here?"

"My grandfather lost touch after he moved, so I'm going to try to find out."

The evening soon came to an end and instructions were given on where to meet up the next day.

Ella awoke to clear blue skies and glorious sunshine. She dressed in shorts and the new polo shirt she'd been given, embossed with the volunteer project's logo, and headed to the meeting point.

Claire and another volunteer were

dishing out the duties for the day.

"We work in pairs," she said. "The tourists are mostly receptive and are completely on board, but you do get the odd few that don't like being told to move away from nesting sites when they're already settled on their towels. Ella, if you can team up with George?"

Ella felt a flutter in her chest and struggled to control the broad smile spreading across her face. He smiled too, and she hoped he was as pleased as her.

"Collecting rubbish today. It may not sound too glamorous but it's very important we keep the beaches clean. The duties will be rotated so don't worry, you won't be on rubbish duty all of the time," Claire said as she handed them black bin bags and pick-up sticks.

"We'll also rota the night duties. No more than two a week – we need everyone fully alert."

Lena questioned what they would be doing on night duty.

"We'll be patrolling the beach. The turtles usually swim ashore during the night to dig in the sand to lay their eggs. We need to watch and place canopies over any nesting sites before people arrive on the beach the following day."

Everyone nodded enthusiastically, realising the importance of this task.

George and Ellen spent their day

"It's laziness, but it's worse when they bury it in the sand and we can't see it."

Claire had been right, most people were genuinely interested and were intrigued by the little wooden canopies placed over the nesting grounds.

They reminded people not to plunge their umbrella poles into the sand anywhere near a nesting area.

"If you push sun umbrellas into the soft sand, they can puncture an egg and then the whole nest will perish," George explained to a group of teenagers.

At the end of the day, George walked Ella back to her apartment. They chatted about their day and what they might be tasked with in the days to come.

"I'm off into Zante Town on my day off, see if I can't find anything out." George hesitated, and stopped walking. "Would you like to come with me? We could grab some lunch by the harbour."

"Yes please, I'd like that."

It hadn't been difficult for George to track down someone who knew his family. The local tavernas were usually passed down the family, and it was the same tradition with the fishing industry.

They ambled along the harbour speaking with as many people as they could. Most could speak English, but those who couldn't, understood what

"You do get the odd few who don't like being told to move away from nests"

walking the length of Lagana Bay picking up rubbish left lying around. Ella was amazed at the amount they collected.

"I don't understand it. Why don't people just put it in the bins? There are plenty about," she commented to Claire when they returned to base with yet another full bag.

George meant when he pointed to a boat and said his surname, Angelopoulos.

They spoke to one fisherman, who was busy unloading his day's catch.

"Ah, Dionissis Agelopoulos – his brother's family still run the Vasilis Taverna further up the harbour front."

George held out his hand to ➤

help Ella down the steep steps to the lower harbour edge where most of the restaurants were situated. She linked her fingers through his and he didn't let go as they walked towards the Vasilis Taverna.

The salty smell of the octopuses draped out to dry filled their nostrils. The scents of fresh lemon and garlic hung in the air as the many restaurants prepared their lunch menus.

Once at the taverna, they explained who George was and he was embraced by the whole family.

His great-uncle hugged him tightly, kissing him on both cheeks.

He called out to the kitchen, beckoning his wife to come out to meet George and a petite woman emerged. She wiped her hands on the front of her apron, before holding out her hand.

"Kalimera," she said in a quiet voice.

George ignored the outstretched hand and hugged her close.

He was introduced to his second cousins and their children, who swarmed around this new and exciting visitor.

They concluded that George and Ella

departing, the younger children running after them along the promenade, waving and shouting "Ya soo."

"Thank you for today," George said as they headed back to the bus stop. "It's been so good to discover I still have family on the island."

"I'm so glad for you, I've had such an amazing day."

His hand tightened around hers and he reached down and gently brushed his lips against hers. "So have I."

The summer months flew by, and they spent their days on the beaches, confidence growing as they became more knowledgeable about the Caretta. They manned the kiosks set around the Bay, handing out leaflets and answering questions from interested tourists.

They spent their night duties lying together in the dunes, hidden by the tall reeds, watching and waiting. Flashlights were forbidden so they relied solely on their night vision.

Excitement rose each time they spotted a Caretta surging out of the waves

They spent their night duties lying together in the dunes, watching

were together, and George did nothing to correct them. Goosebumps popped up along Ella's arms and she felt a delicious shiver of delight.

They were treated to a feast of Greek Meze, fresh fish and garlic roast potatoes for lunch. They drank ouzo and heard tales of their families and what the brothers had got up to together when they were younger.

After several hours it was time for them to leave. They hugged and kissed every member of the family before

onto the sand and making her way to the spot where she had been born.

"I just can't believe they know exactly where to go," she whispered.

As soon as the Caretta was back in the water they crept down and popped a canopy over the site, complete with a tag indicating the time and date so they would have a rough idea when the hatchlings would attempt their journey to the sea.

Later in the season, they watched nervously as the hatchlings exited their nests and tried to follow the reflection of the moonlight on the water. Any artificial lights shining from the back of the beach could confuse them. Claire had warned the volunteers that they were never allowed to touch or pick up the hatchlings to help them to the sea; they needed to track the characteristics of the beach so they could return as adults to make their own nests.

Ella sucked in a deep breath, clasping her hand over her mouth as she watched the hatchlings fumble their way towards the water's edge.

"Go on, you can do it."

She gripped George's hand as their bodies snaked along the sand.

With one final surge, the last tiny turtle made it and it was only then that Ella realised she'd been holding her breath.

"They've made it," she said, wiping her forearm across her face.

The holiday season was drawing to an end, signalling a drop in the people using the beaches. Most of the volunteers would stay in Zante until mid-November, before returning home. Some would stay on further and get casual work helping to harvest the olives.

Ella knew the time was drawing closer for her return flight. They hadn't spoken about leaving; she and George both knew that they were too far apart for a long distance relationship.

Ella wanted to return the following March and help out before starting uni. Yet she knew it wouldn't be the same without George.

She thought she had her life planned, and chosen a course that would ensure she had a good job at the end of her degree, but that was now up for debate. Her time in Zante had created a fresh new outlook on life for her, and she now found she wanted to research courses in environmental studies. She discussed her ideas with George and he encouraged her to go with her heart.

The day before her flight was a sombre time for Ella. She would miss the island, of course, and working with the volunteering group – but they faded into insignificance when she compared her feelings to how much she would miss George.

"Will you come back?" she asked him.

"I think my family may want to take a trip out here once I tell them about the relatives I've found." He turned to face Ella, averting his eyes from hers, afraid of what his own would do. "But it wouldn't be the same without you here."

Hot tears pooled in the corners of Ella's eyes, and a blink sent them sliding down her cheeks, before dropping onto the sand by her feet.

George lifted his hand and his thumb glided across her face, brushing away the sun-kissed strands of hair clinging to her dampened skin.

"I've been thinking that I should also follow my heart." He paused before continuing. "The UK has some great universities where I could continue my environmental studies."

Ella tilted her gaze and her eyebrows lifted. She reached up and put her arms around his neck, and pulled him towards her. Her lips touched his, before moving close to his ear.

"Actually, I think I can recommend the perfect one." Ⓜ

Coronation Chicken Gems

Ingredients (Makes approx. 18)

- **4tbsp mayonnaise**
- **4tbsp Greek style natural yogurt**
- **2tsp medium curry powder**
- **300g roast chicken breast, chopped**
- **50g ready-to-eat dried apricots, chopped**
- **50g sultanas**
- **Salt and freshly ground black pepper**
- **Little Gem lettuce leaves**
- **Chopped tomato and chives, to garnish**

1 Mix together the mayonnaise, yogurt and curry powder. Add the chicken, the apricots and sultanas. Season and stir well.

2 Spoon the mixture into the Little Gem lettuce leaves, then garnish with tomato and chives. Keep chilled until ready to serve.

RECIPES AND FOOD STYLING: SUE ASHWORTH PHOTOGRAPHY: JONATHAN SHORT

Kriss Kross

Try to fit all the listed words back into the grid.

4 letters	7 letters	9 letters	11 letters
KINK	CASSOCK	FIRELIGHT	DESTINATION
OURS	SCRUFFY	HOLLYHOCK	MERCHANDISE
5 letters	**8 letters**	**10 letters**	UNINITIATED
FOIST	CHENILLE	BANDLEADER	
SHAFT	SHAMEFUL	EQUANIMITY	
WEALD			

Codeword

Each letter of the alphabet has been replaced by a number. The numbers for the first name of our chosen celebrity are given. Complete the puzzle to reveal which Nepal animals TV host Liz Bonnin tracked as part of her Master's Degree in wild animal biology.

20	5	1	20	4	4	13	8	20	7	6		7 L	13 I	26 Z
14		11		13		21		17		2		13		11
19	20	15	13	20		1	22	20	4	1	20	15	14	11
20		10		19		12				12		20		23
14	2	9	18	20	14		13	15	13	21	13	2	21	20
		20								4		19		20
1	9	22	7	6						3	20	20	24	
11														20
15	13	1	23							21	9	21	11	22
25		22		24								11		
7	20	2	8	20	15	20	14		9	4	9	22	24	4
13		4		14				21		2		15		12
1	2	4	21	2	17	2	6	4		16	20	2	21	6
21		7		7		4		2		18		14		7
4	7	6		11	18	4	20	22	8	2	21	11	22	6

A B C D E F G H I̷ J K L̷ M N O P Q R S T U V W X Y Z̷

| 1 | 2 | 3 | 4 | 5 | 6 | 7 L | 8 | 9 | 10 | 11 | 12 | 13 I |
| 14 | 15 | 16 | 17 | 18 | 19 | 20 | 21 | 22 | 23 | 24 | 25 | 26 Z |

Turn To P171-173 For Solutions

| 21 | 13 I | 19 | 20 | 22 | 4 |

The Bookshop Mystery

At the pirate-themed fair, there were as many interesting characters in real life as in Cassie's books...

By H Johnson-Mack

Cassie smiled to herself as she pegged back the door of her mobile bookshop then positioned a set of steps firmly in place. The early morning was promising to develop into a beautiful day; just a hint of a breeze and clouds already dispersing to reveal bolts of azure blue sky.

"Perfect weather so far, Luna," she said to her scruffy cross-breed spaniel. "With any luck, we'll get that beach walk I promised you."

After a day's successful selling, she thought hopefully, stepping into the converted one-storey bus, her smile slipping just a touch. She never regretted leaving the nine-to-five working life and investing the money her gran had left in this dream of a mobile bookshop, Other Worlds Inside. But there were times when she struggled to make ends meet.

Luckily, she had an unfailing love of books and travelling, and a supportive family, so she never lost faith for long. Besides, today's event, eagerly anticipated within the Norfolk neighbourhood she'd been residing in this weekend, would surely bring the crowds and thus some custom her way. For who could resist sitting in the sun with a good book?

She was still installing her awning with book nook beneath when her next-door pitch neighbour arrived in a battered Land Rover. He raised a hand in greeting, which Cassie returned, watching him for longer than necessary as he set up his stall.

It wasn't just the items he was unveiling – beautifully modelled twisty metalwork – that caught her eye. The guy himself was interesting, too, with conker-brown hair, muscular arms and a strange half-apron slung round his hips.

He installed workbench, clamps and stool at the front of his pitch, with what looked like a menacing soldering iron hung from one side. Glancing up, he saw her watching and sent her a lopsided grin.

"Do you have a licence for that

Her habit of matching people to a book character seemed to have deserted her

contraption?" she asked cheekily, wandering nearer.

"She can get pretty hot but her bark's worse than her bite," he assured her. "It's how I make the metal curve into some of these creations, the simpler ones."

"They're very good."

"Thanks. I'm Finn, by the way."

"Cassie," she returned, smiling,

shaking the hand he held out to her.

"Short for?"

"Cassiopeia. My mum has a thing for astrology." She smiled at his involuntary grimace. "I know. It could have been worse, I suppose. Do you have time for a brew before the hordes descend?"

"Always." Finn followed her across to her pitch. "Nice place. I don't suppose you've got any David Gemmell fantasy fiction in your collection?" He hesitated at sight of Luna, who gave a warning growl.

"Don't worry." Cassie ruffled the dog's grey-and-black head. "Her bark's worse than her bite too."

Finn was helping Cassie to fix some fabric bunting around her pitch when one of the event organisers came by with a list of the day's events.

"Big draw and chest opening at four pm," the sleek woman whose name badge proclaimed her as Dorian announced. "You can stay on site until six."

Cassie resisted an urge to salute.

"What exactly is in the chest?" Finn wondered as Dorian left.

Cassie shrugged.

"Well, as this is a pirate's festival to honour the old Smugglers Inn on the headland, I'm guessing they want people to believe it's some kind of contraband."

"That's worth the purchase of some raffle tickets, I think. I'll get you a couple, too, as a thanks for the tea."

Cassie watched Finn saunter off through the sprouting mushrooms of stalls and fluttering banners dotting the site. Funny, but her habit of matching anyone she found interesting to a character from a book had appeared to desert her where this guy was concerned. Was he *Rebecca*'s brooding Maxim de Winter, or more of a dashing Valencourt from Mrs Radcliffe's *Mysteries of Udolpho*? Too soon to tell.

Well, she'd work it out sooner or later. Now it was time to sell some stories. ➤

To her delight, the field soon began to buzz with folk and four-legged friends, some of whom caused Luna to be a little too vocal in her efforts for attention. Cassie settled her down in a favourite cushioned spot within the van, and went back outside to welcome everyone into her little emporium.

Dorian's itinerary listed morning activities as Morris dancing and nautical games, which included a pirate plank competition. Cassie was serenaded by a unique mash-up of flutes, bells and Taylor Swift-style pop as she sold a selection of crime and classics to new customers, including a dripping young Plank contestant who reminded her of Pippi Longstocking.

She'd had hardly any time to indulge in her own selection of summer reading, stashed in her Mary-Poppins deep tapestry bag. But that was a good thing, for it meant business was brisk.

She was just contemplating the tuna and cucumber sandwiches waiting for her lunch when a portly man sidled up the bookshop steps. Was it because one of the stories she was currently reading was *David Copperfield* that she immediately thought of the eternal optimist Mr Micawber from that tale? More likely, the velveteen waistcoat and paisley scarf had influenced her!

She watched, ostensibly fussing over Luna, as he prowled around, scanning the bookshelves. It was always intriguing to try and guess what type of tale would appeal to individuals, but blinded by her character match, she couldn't get past Victorian literature with this man.

He didn't seem sure of what he liked, either, as he occasionally selected a thick volume from a shelf, only to push it back again. He glanced her way and cleared his throat. Cassie, feeling she might be making him uncomfortable, took Luna and left him to it. When he finally emerged with a book in hand, his choice made her smile. *The Thirty-Nine Steps.*

"I'm… humph… keen on this old hardback," he said, not quite meeting her eyes. "But it's pretty pricey."

"It's a rare edition," Cassie pointed out, adding silently, *from my Grandad's old collection,* "so I have to sell it for a little more than other stock."

The man considered, gaze darting side to side, then pushed the book into her hands. "Fair enough. Would you hold this back for me for a few hours? I think I do want it but I need to look around first."

"No problem. I'll do that," Cassie promised, tucking the book behind her little counter.

Thanking her, he hurried away, leaving her pondering. The book wasn't that expensive, not compared to others she'd seen – even bought – that were classed as rare. Thoughtful now, she rummaged in her bag for her laptop and sandwich in hand, took a trip online in search of more books like her grandad's Buchan, which resulted in her phoning an old friend.

Hey, neighbour." Cassie was dragged out of Dickens' *Copperfield* world by Finn's voice. "The lunchtime lull gives me an excuse for a wander. Paul next to me has agreed to keep an eye on my stall, so d'you fancy closing yours up and coming for a walk?"

"Yes, please. Luna would love that."

Even as Cassie rose, a flustered Dorian, flanked by a tall policewoman introduced simply as Jas, intercepted them.

"There's been an incident," she

declared, the morning's strident tones completely dampened. When she failed to elaborate, Jas took up the tale.

"The key to the prize chest has gone missing. So we're searching the area and asking stallholders if they've seen anything unusual or a man dressed as…" She coughed. "Long John Silver. I appreciate you can only glimpse the chest plinth from here, but we need to check just in case."

Finn and Cassie shook their heads, Cassie adding, "Nothing, I'm afraid." The policewoman extended her fingers to Luna.

"Well, if we could ask you to be vigilant and let us know if anything turns up. Hello, gorgeous."

With that sweet parting shot to her surprisingly docile dog, Cassie watched the pair move on to Paul and his botanical beauty stall.

Finn exhaled a sigh. "Looks like those tickets will be worthless, then. I wonder what's in the chest that would make someone steal the key to unlock it?"

"Ooh, a real live mystery, with a pirate villain!" Cassie would have rubbed her hands together if she weren't holding Luna's leash in one. "How delicious."

"You like a puzzle?"

"Doesn't everyone?" she enthused. "After all, some of the best characters in

A crowd had gathered round the prize chest plinth. Cassie held Luna back from shuffling feet as Finn asked the man on guard if the key had been recovered.

"Not yet, though the police have stop-searched four Long John Silvers."

"Why them?" Cassie wondered.

"The key went missing during the Pirate Plank final, when this place was unattended. A few people said they saw a guy dressed as Silver hanging round at the time. But it could have been anyone. Bit stupid of the organisers to leave the key in a box under here."

Cassie frowned as he gestured to a broken case discarded by the red tablecloth draping the plinth.

"But who would have known that the key was there?"

The guard shrugged.

"It wasn't a secret. Obviously, someone didn't want to rely just on luck to get the prize."

Long John Silver…" Cassie mused as Finn set a cloudy lemonade on the café table before her. "Bit too obvious, don't you think?"

Finn studied her in a way that set her stomach fluttering.

"The bad sailor after more than his fair share of treasure."

"Looks like our tickets will be worthless, then. I wonder what's in the chest"

storytelling are from the pages of crime."

"So you're off to search for this Long John Silver? Channel your inner Marple?"

"More like Nancy Drew," said Cassie. "She's the one who always uncovered hidden treasure."

"Well, then, Nancy, let's see what we can find. And let's pick up something from a food van along the way; I'm starving."

"I think so. If I was to cast a character for a play of this kind, he'd be my immediate… Wait a minute. 'Anyone acting strangely,' the police said. That makes me think of Micawber."

"Excuse me?"

Cassie flushed.

"Oh, it's a habit of mine; I liken anyone interesting I meet to story ➤

characters. Anyway, this Mr Micawber was in my bookshop earlier, acting furtively. Now I wonder why. That pocketed waistcoat of his could easily hide a key or two."

"So, what character did you come up with for me?"

She avoided Finn's eyes as she said, "I couldn't read you, actually."

"Really?"

"Well, I… oh!" Cassie's sudden jump from her seat sent the snoozing Luna tumbling across her toes. "Finn, the book!"

M icawber wanted me to keep one aside for him, as he couldn't decide whether to buy it or not," she explained as they hurried back to her van, Luna eagerly leading the way.

"Wow – how much were you charging for it? Ten doubloons?"

"Normal price for an old hardback, so it was odd he didn't just buy it. But then, he did seem distracted."

"You think he could have tucked the key inside the book?"

"It would explain his weird behaviour, don't you think?"

But to her intense disappointment, when Cassie tore open the book, it was

With a triumphant shout, she tugged a volume from its slot then gave a gasp of horror as the pages fell open and a shower of jagged pieces scattered, confetti-like, over the floor. Finn was at her side, ready to catch the book as she stumbled backward, hand on chest.

"You've found it!" he breathed, staring at the old key cut into the pages, then tilted the volume to read the spine. "*Treasure Island.* Unbelievable! Or very clever. Who would ever guess that a thief would be so clichéed?"

"He's destroyed the book," Cassie was moaning. "That's sacrilege!"

"I'm sorry about that," Finn said. "But look on the bright side. At least you've solved the mystery."

Cassie sniffed. "Hardly worth the loss of an illustrated Louis Stevenson, is it?"

T he authorities didn't agree. Dorian was clearly delighted, until the police requested that they refrain from revealing the key's discovery right away.

"We need to give the thief a chance to collect it," the dog-loving policewoman Jas pointed out, with a sidelong look of raised brows at Cassie. She added, "If you're willing to assist us?"

She gave a gasp of horror. A shower of jagged pieces scattered to the floor

depressingly intact and ordinary.

"Never mind, Miss Drew," Finn consoled her. "It's not that easy to uncover treasure."

"Treasure…" Cassie repeated thoughtfully, then laughed aloud. "Oh, no, surely not!"

"What?" Finn demanded as she shot across to her Classics shelf and ran her fingers frantically along the multi-coloured and textured spines.

Cassie nodded, still mentally kicking herself for leaving a suspicious person unattended in her shop.

Finn nudged her and grinned.

"Nancy Drew, eat your heart out."

T he afternoon seemed to slide by at a snail's pace, though Cassie was busy enough. Ordinarily, she would be really pleased with the number of customers Other Worlds saw, but she was so on edge for any sign of Micawber she couldn't relax to enjoy it.

When he finally did return, she almost missed him, being engaged in an animated sale with a woman who wanted four romances for the price of one. Luckily, Jas was more observant and intercepted him with impressive understated elegance as he withdrew *Treasure Island* from the shelf. Cassie hastily gathered Luna to her chest in case the dog decided to join in Jas's game.

Unfortunately for Micawber, he had his hand on the key just as Jas challenged him and wasn't quick enough with an excuse to avoid being led away for questioning, ruined book and all.

So, did you get your half-book back?" Finn asked a little later, setting out a folding chair for her beside his own in view of the chest plinth.

"Umm, plus a thank you for my help." Cassie sighed and sipped disconsolately at the steaming cup of tea she held. "It's ruined, of course."

"You could always put it on display, to get your customers in the mood for a funny mystery adventure."

"Good idea." Cassie's smile returned. "Micawber did do me a favour, actually. His casual comment on rare books got me thinking about a new stand, and I've been talking to a friend of mine who deals in such volumes. It could be a good sideline for me. Oh, and I asked whether he had any good Gemmells in store."

"And has he?"

"Yes, he does, but they come with a certain condition –"

Before Finn could respond, a huge drumroll boomed from the loudspeakers, and Dorian's voice announced it was finally time for the prize raffle. Finn and Cassie produced their tickets with a mix of excitement and hope, which gradually dimmed as the winning numbers were called out, matching none of theirs.

"Oh, well," said Finn as a lady in a poppy-bright dress flew forward, waving a ticket. "Better luck next time. I wonder what she's won."

Cassie held her breath as the key was handed over and with a flourish, Poppy-Lady unlocked the chest.

Dorian greeted the unveiling of its contents – little more than a fancy hamper with some chocolate coins – as though she were staring at a crock of gold. Cassie and Finn exchanged glances.

"Not quite pirate's treasure," Cassie observed. "Why on earth our funny Micawber wanted that, I'll never know."

Finn laughed. "Perhaps he's a sucker for paté de foie gras. Anyway," he said, sobering, "what was this condition you were just about to tell me about?"

Cassie's cheeks bloomed in a gentle blush and she smiled coyly.

"Well, my friend's going to send me the books, but that'll take some time. So we'll have to exchange phone numbers, and meet up again, if you want them."

Finn's grin was slow and, to Cassie, utterly irresistible.

"No problem. In the meantime, there's that nice infamous Smugglers Inn just down the road. How about I take you and Luna to dinner and see if by evening's end, you can work out what story character I remind you of?"

Cassie's smile was pure gold.

"It's a date." Ⓜ

Missing Link

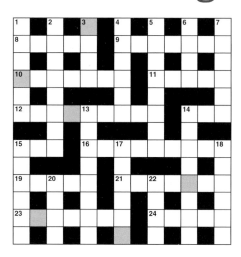

The answer to each clue is a word which has a link with each of the three words listed. This word may come at the end (eg **HEAD** linked with **BEACH, BIG, HAMMER**), at the beginning (eg **BLACK** linked with **BEAUTY, BOARD and JACK**) or a mixture of the two (eg **STONE** linked with **HAIL, LIME and WALL**).

ACROSS

8 Boy, Physics, Turf (5)
9 Blood, Jaffa, Seville (7)
10 Rules, Sanctions, Upon (7)
11 Flowering, Garden, Lemon (5)
12 Double, High, Trading (9)
14 Cat, Cruise, Thumb (3)
15 Berg, Cube, Pack (3)
16 Cream, Lotion, Palate (9)
19 Market, New, Shanty (5)
21 Matches, Tents, Wildcat (7)
23 Cover, Neckline, Surgery (7)
24 Barn, Dinner, Hall (5)

DOWN

1 Bad, Eating, Old (6)
2 Production, Time, Work (8)
3 Big, Tip, Twinkle (4)
4 Guard, Herbaceous, Line (6)
5 Politics, Ship, Yugoslav (8)
6 Duckling, Scene, Sisters (4)
7 High, Public, Self (6)
13 Landmark, Makers, Tree (8)
14 Aloud, Cap, Lateral (8)
15 Calorie, Food, Sharp (6)
17 Bonnet, Egg, Parade (6)
18 Choir, Singer, Truth (6)
20 Edge, Length, Separate (4)
22 Bus, Fairground, Free (4)

Hidden word in the shaded squares: _____

Sudoku

			9			4	3	
				7	2			
6	1						5	
9			5	6				1
1		8			6			5
5			8	4				7
	5					8	3	
			7	2				
	9	6			8			

Fill in each of the blank squares with the numbers 1 to 9, so that each row, each column and each 3x3 cell contains all the numbers from 1 to 9.

Word Wheel

Turn To P171-173 For Solutions

You have ten minutes to find as many words as possible using the letters in the wheel. Each word must be three letters or more and contain the central letter. Use each letter once and no plurals, foreign words or proper nouns are allowed. There is at least one nine-letter word.

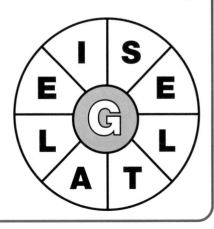

Average: 32 words
Good: 33-48 words
Excellent: 49-63 words

The Wedding

Just what was it about her sister's third marriage that had got up her nose – and what would she do about it?

By Valerie Bowes

W hy put that in the window? Not exactly a come-and-get-me, was it? Although she might be a tad biased. Molly looked at the shop-window dummy with disfavour. OK, so it was an animal charity, not a high-end dress shop, but surely they could find something with a bit more oomph and display it better than that?

The skirt was pinned untidily so it sagged around the model's waist and the blouse they'd teamed it with was anything but inspiring. Who would put beige with a grey skirt and jacket? Especially a beige as limp and lifeless as that. Molly shook her head and hurried away. No use mooning over an outfit in a charity shop window when she had shopping to do, Bill's library book to take back, and dinner to make.

Anyway, with a bit of luck it would be

She'd fallen for the drape of the fabric and the fit of the jacket. It would have been great for a normal wedding, teamed with a vibrant blouse and a spectacular hat, but Bill had been right. Sophie wouldn't have a normal wedding.

"Grey? For Sophie's wedding? Come on, love. Your sister's not going to be in the traditional white meringue, is she? She's probably going to wear a dress you need sunglasses to look at."

"She might have in her hippy days," retorted Molly. "In fact, I know she did. I was there, remember? A kaftan and a flowing headband, if I remember rightly. But that was nearly fifty years ago. She's got more sense now."

Bill snorted. "I wouldn't bank on it. This is Sophie we're talking about! And she is getting married for the third time."

"Yes, right."

She wasn't going to her sister's wedding because it was being held in Thailand

gone the next time she came through the precinct. The animals in the local shelter needed feeding and looking after. That's why she'd given it to them in the first place.

No, not quite the first place. Bill had put the doubts into her mind.

Molly remembered her sister's previous weddings. Mary Quant miniskirt, white tights, and floppy-brimmed purple hat for the first, and that zinging yellow kaftan for the second.

"Mikey lasted under a year, and she walked out on Wayne when Tricia was only eight. Anyway, she can wear what she likes. I'm not going looking as if I'm dressed for a Sixties Evening. This outfit is classy." She didn't add *and it's more suitable for my age* but the thought did

flash across her mind. She shoved it away with a shudder.

"But… grey?" Bill shook his head.

Molly scowled at him and took the costume upstairs to hang it in the wardrobe. She liked it, and she'd wear what she wanted, even if Sophie disapproved. But her sister was bound to choose something a bit more suitable than the last two… wasn't she?

The words mutton and lamb drifted through her mind.

Well, that wasn't going to apply to her.

The grey costume was still in the window the next time she went to the shops. If anything, it looked worse than the first time she'd seen it. Someone had piled a few assorted jigsaws around the model's feet and leant a particularly uninspiring picture against them, pressing into the skirt.

However, someone would buy it, and the animals would get the benefit. It was no use to her. She wasn't going to any wedding, grey outfit or not. And why wasn't she going to her sister's wedding? Because it was going to be on a beach in Thailand, that's why.

Molly had nearly blown a gasket when Sophie told her.

"What's wrong with the Registry Office here? Or The Castle? That's got a wedding license now and it's ➡

spectacular enough even for you. It's got battlements and everything."

"Yes, it's beautiful. It could be on the cover of any glossy magazine – probably is – but it's not what we want."

"Too conventional, I suppose," Molly said, trying to keep the exasperation out of her voice. "Too… normal."

Sophie giggled, proving she'd hit the nail on the head.

"We're going to have a simple wedding on the beach. Not loads of people. Just family and a few friends."

"What about Tricia? Doesn't she have a say in it?"

"Oh, she's giving me away," Sophie said sunnily.

"I'll bet she's offering a discount," Molly muttered.

"And Regan and Kia are bridesmaids."

How would Regan and Kia feel about that? Molly wondered. It would be odd enough being bridesmaid to your grannie,

evening, she told Bill about Sophie's wedding. "We're not going, of course."

To her surprise, he actually seemed disappointed. "Sounds a nice idea to me, getting married on a beach. Saves all that dressing up. And uncomfortable shoes. Anyway, I think you'd both look great in sarongs, actually."

"Oh, very funny," Molly said, suspecting sarcasm. "She assures me she won't be wearing one, and Andrew won't be wearing budgie-smugglers. But not because they're sticking to a bridal gown and morning suit. Oh no, they're going to be wearing wet-suits, because they're going diving afterwards!

"They're laying on a nice picnic for the rest of us and we can chill on the beach or swim if we want to."

Molly's tone made it plain what she thought of that idea.

"Well, I think it sounds wonderful."

Molly couldn't believe her ears. How

The hat lasted longer than the marriage and now she's getting married again

never mind about doing it in bare feet and hoping your carefully wrapped sarong didn't fall off.

"Sorry, Sophie, you'll just have to manage without Bill and me. Going all the way to Thailand just for a wedding? It's ridiculous!"

"It's your decision, but I'd really like you to be there."

It sounded as if Sophie really meant it, but Molly wasn't falling for emotional blackmail. That

could Bill think it was a good idea, let alone call it wonderful? But he wouldn't be moved from his standpoint and they had a regular slanging match, a thing they rarely did.

Which was why she'd packed up the skirt and jacket the next day and marched down to the shop with it.

Now, here it was, three weeks away from the wedding and the outfit was still staring her accusingly in the face every time she went shopping. It looked greyer and duller every time.

Especially today. The damp and gloomy weather was doing its best to make everyone feel down, one of the lights in the charity shop window was on the blink and Molly couldn't stop thinking about sun, sea and sarongs. This was all wrong. It had to stop.

She went up to the shop door and gave it a vigorous shove. A harrassed-looking woman looked up from sorting through a pile of clothes that Molly wouldn't have used for dusters.

"Can I help you?"

"Yes," Molly said. "I'd like to buy that skirt and jacket in the window. Don't worry about trying it on. I know it fits."

She stared around while the woman wrestled the skirt off the model. Sprawling heaps of things were lumped haphazardly everywhere.

"You look as if you could do with some help in this shop," she said.

"Tell me about it!" the woman said with fervour. "I've lost my two best assistants recently. Jane was great at doing the window, but I haven't got her gift, I'm afraid."

"Would I do? I worked in a dress shop."

The words were out before she knew she was going to say them. It was Sophie who plunged in recklessly, not her. And, although it was the truth, it had been as a Saturday girl when she was 15.

"I don't know how good I'll be, but I'll give it a go."

"You can't be worse than me. When can you start?" It was plain the woman could have hugged her.

"Now? I could spare you an hour." She had nothing else lined up, did she?

"Oh, wonderful! Are you sure? Can you help me sort this lot? Not that there's anything very good here – well, I haven't found anything, anyway. My name's Alice, by the way."

"Molly. Pleased to meet you."

As she began to lift and fold garments, a flash of purple caught her eye and she disinterred a floppy felt hat. A ripple of recognition fluttered her stomach.

"That's not bad," said Alice. "We might be able to find a home for that."

"My sister wore one like this at her first wedding," Molly said, twirling it on her finger. "It lasted longer than the marriage did and now she's getting married again."

She'd thought people would regard any sister of hers as a bit long in the tooth to be thinking of romance, but Alice beamed.

"Good for her! Do tell her congratulations from me."

"Thanks," Molly said awkwardly. She set the hat aside but, while her hands moved automatically, her thoughts were far away.

What was it about Sophie's wedding that had got up her nose? Why didn't she want to go? The marriages to Mikey and Wayne hadn't lasted, but Molly didn't think that would happen with Andrew. He was a really nice guy and he clearly adored her sister. And, let's face it, neither of them were spring chickens. ➜

Surely they should be capable of making right choices by now? It wasn't that she was jealous, either. She was perfectly happy with her Bill.

So what was her problem?

The problem was that there was no problem. No reason at all why she shouldn't go. It had been an automatic response to Sophie's flamboyance. Still, after all these years.

It was time she stopped being afraid people would think she was trying to copy her older sister and not being as good at it. Maybe it was time to release her own unconventional side. It sounded as if Bill would be all for it.

She'd start right now.

A small tsunami of excitement swept all her doubts aside. She glanced around at the shop. That depressing rail of limp trousers would have to be jazzed up somehow and the crowded shelves of knicknacks thinned out and displayed to much better advantage.

It was going to be fun, shaking this place into life. Give her own life a new purpose and the animals would benefit.

Alice was clearly good at the admin stuff, but she needed someone to help her. Molly felt her

creative juices, so long unused, begin to stir. It was a win-win.

So was a trip to Thailand. Sophie wanted her and Bill at this wedding, so she'd get her wish. Molly's thoughts were busy as she folded and sorted. She put a final shabby skirt on the reject pile and sat back.

"Right, Alice, I have to go now, but I'll be back tomorrow, after some shopping for the wedding."

She tucked the grey costume under her arm and hurried off. An electric blue top she'd had her eye on would go beautifully with this silvery fabric, but that would be for other occasions.

She needed a pedicure if she was going barefoot. And a floaty dress. She didn't think her figure would accommodate sarong and swimming cozzies and she wasn't much of a swimmer, but a sundress would be great for a beach wedding. No tasteful pastel stripes or florals, either. She was going to go for sizzling orange – the brighter, the better. **MW**

A sundress would be perfect – and no tasteful pastels, but sizzling orange!

Puff Pastry Baked Egg Tart

Ingredients (Serves 4)

- **500g puff pastry**
- **1tbsp plain flour**
- **4tbsp pesto sauce**
- **12 baby tomatoes, thickly sliced**
- **280g mozzarella minis, drained and halved**
- **4 small eggs**
- **Few fresh basil leaves, to garnish**
- **Freshly ground black pepper**

1 Preheat the oven to 200°C, Fan180°C, Gas 6. Roll out the pastry on a lightly floured surface to a 30cm square. Cut into 4 even squares. Place on two baking trays. Score a 1cm border around the edge of each. Spread the centre with pesto sauce,

2 Arrange the tomatoes and mozzarella around the edges, leaving the space in the middle empty. Bake for 10mins, crack an egg into the centre of each tart and return to the oven for 6-8mins, until the egg white is set.

3 Serve immediately, garnished with fresh basil leaves and sprinkled with freshly ground black pepper. Serve with a green salad.

700 calories per square

RECIPES AND FOOD STYLING: JENNIE SHAPTER
PHOTOGRAPHY: JON WHITAKER

Money Matters

In the battle of the generations, will progress or tradition triumph? Or might Lynn and Hollie agree to differ?

By Anne Thompson

Ｗe'll be a cashless society in a few years," Hollie said to her mother, Lynn, as they walked along the street on one of their regular shopping trips.

"Nonsense!" Lynn replied. "We might be using cards for expensive things now, but we'll still need cash for little things."

"No, we won't!" came the answer.

Just as they rounded the corner, they saw a young man selling The Big Issue. As if to prove her point, Hollie went up to him, took a copy and paid by holding her debit card to his card reader.

Lynn sighed. Hollie had become so anti-cash since she had started working for a bank a few years ago. It was true that it wasn't a good idea to walk round with a lot of cash in your purse, but Lynn still felt

"Yes – and before you say I won't be able to buy anything with a card, my friend Jasmine told me they've got three or four card readers ready!"

Lynn decided to change the subject.

"How much stuff have you got for the baby?" she asked.

"A few bits and pieces," Hollie replied, patting her large tummy. "But I'm hoping for some nice stuff at the baby shower in a couple of weeks!"

Later, at the shopping mall, she tried on a few maternity clothes.

"I think I'll take this," she said, holding on to a brightly-coloured sweatshirt. As they made their way to the till, there was some kind of commotion among the staff.

"I'm awfully sorry," the girl behind the counter said, "but the computer's gone down. I'm afraid we can't accept any

"That's ridiculous! He could be spending hundreds of pounds on sweets"

that it was always prudent to have a small amount handy.

They arrived at their favourite coffee shop and placed their order. It was Hollie's turn to pay, so she got out her credit card and then they sat down.

"There's a jumble sale for charity in the church hall this week," Lynn said. "Are you planning to go?"

card payments just at the moment."

"Will this do?" Lynn asked, whipping a twenty-pound note out of her handbag and looking at her daughter smugly.

"Certainly, madam – but I can only give you a hand-written receipt."

"Fine," Lynn said, putting the receipt away and trying not to laugh.

"Well, that was only a fluke," Hollie

PICTURES: SHUTTERSTOCK

78 www.myweekly.co.uk

protested. "How often does something like that happen?"

"Often enough to make it worthwhile having some cash," he mother muttered. "Anyway, when the baby's big enough to count, you'll have to give him or her a bit of cash as pocket money."

"Rubbish! It'll have its own little credit card!"

"Seriously?"

"Of course! It'll learn just as well as when you taught me with Toytown money in that little shop I used to play with."

"But –" Lynn stopped short as her daughter gave her a sudden nudge.

"Look! You see that kid over there,"

Lynn followed her gaze and noticed a boy aged about ten paying for a bag of sweets by using his smartphone.

"But that's ridiculous!" she snapped. "He could be spending hundreds of pounds on sweets and ice-cream, for all his parents know!"

"But the parents can top it up with a certain amount every day, or however often they want. That way, he can't go on a spending spree!"

"Hmm," Lynn grumbled. "Well, I still think you can't beat good old-fashioned pocket money."

"Oh, Mum, your grandchild's going to grow up in a cashless world!"

On the way home, they stopped for petrol at the local garage which had been run by the same family for many years.

"Oh no!" Hollie exclaimed, reading a notice on the pump. "Their terminal's down as well! They wouldn't take cash for as much petrol as we want to buy, even if I had any notes!"

"Just a minute," Lynn said, slipping off. After a brief conversation with old Mr. Watson, who seemed to have run the garage ever since his father used to fill the cars himself, Lynn announced, "It's all right! He'll take a cheque!"

"A cheque?" Hollie asked, as if she'd never heard of one before. "Since when do you go around with a cheque book in your handbag?"

"Since yesterday, when I paid my subscription to the History Society and forgot to put the book back in the drawer."

The day of the baby shower arrived at last. Hollie beamed as her friends generously handed her baby clothes and all manner of equipment. Eventually they drifted off and Lynn noticed that one present was still left, unopened.

"You've missed one!" she said, pointing to the beautifully wrapped gift.

"I hadn't forgotten! I'm saving the best till last – that's from Great-Aunt Liz, so it's bound to be something really good and expensive!"

Hollie picked up the parcel, tore off the paper in excitement and then gawped open-mouthed as she pulled out a beautiful, solid silver… money box. **Ⓜ**

Kriss Kross

Try to fit all the listed words back into the grid.

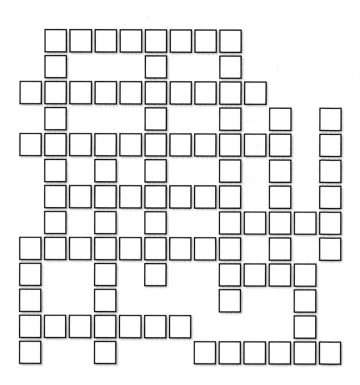

4 letters	**6 letters**	**8 letters**	**10 letters**
ABET	DEMOTE	EVENTING	JUBILATION
AURA	RANDOM	INVESTOR	TRANSISTOR
5 letters	**7 letters**	**9 letters**	**11 letters**
INTRO	PSALTER	DEVIATION	GEOMETRICAL
PADRE	RISOTTO	EDUCATIVE	LADDISHNESS
		PEDAGOGIC	

Codeword

Each letter of the alphabet has been replaced by a number. The numbers for the first name of our chosen celebrity are given. Complete the puzzle to reveal which company both of TV explorer Steve Backshall's parents worked for.

1	19	22	19	12	23	9	19	6	21	16		4	7	12
4		24		13		7		1		12		21		13
20	14	24	13	24		9	8	8	24	5	9	26	14	24
24	**S**	19	**T**	7	**E**	20	**V**		**E**	24		14		7
14	23	24	19	14	16		11	1	21	21	5	12	15	24
		20								20		12		25
6	26	14	24	20						22	19	24	24
12														7
26	8	4	20						18	26	7	26	14
21		24		20								17		
4	12	7	14	26	11	21	24		20	14	7	1	14	20
12		3		2				18		1		11		26
20	10	1	24	26	8	9	20	17		2	7	26	9	21
14		7		7		7		9		14		7		21
20	26	16		9	19	24	25	18	1	20	26	11	21	16

A B C D É F G H I J K L M N O P Q R Ṣ Ṭ U Ṿ W X Y Z

1	2	3	4	5	6	7	8	9	10	11	12	13
												V
14	15	16	17	18	19	20	21	22	23	24	25	26
T						**S**				**E**		

Turn To P171-173 For Solutions

| 11 | 7 | 9 | 14 | 9 | 20 | 17 | | 26 | 9 | 7 | 23 | 26 | 16 | 20 |
| | | | **T** | | **S** | | | | | | | | | **S** |

The Fabric Of Friendship

They'd been friends for thirty years – but would they still be close after this evening's clothes swap party?

By S. Bee

My heart sank when I saw my friend Ros at the party

I thought you couldn't make it?" I greeted my friend Ros as she arrived at the clothes swap party with a bursting Bag for Life.

Yet my heart sank, because I worried that the chances of us recognising garments we'd swapped already between us were pretty high.

"I managed to find a babysitter," she explained. "Weren't you doing something tonight too, Emma?"

"I forgot the book club was taking a break. When the reminder text came in, I came along instead," I explained.

The clothes swap party was being held in my neighbour's house.

Besides helping ourselves to new – or rather new-ish – free clothes, there was also music, and nibbles and drinks were supplied.

As Ros and I chatted,

more guests arrived and had begun to throw their swap garments in a big heap on the carpet. So we did the same.

Five minutes later, as I had predicted, chaos broke out…

"I gave you this, Ros!" I held the gold blouse aloft. "I bought it in the Reynold's sale but when I got it home, I realised it didn't match my outfits. You admired it – so I gave it to you."

Ros reddened. "Oh yes. I remember now," she stammered lamely.

I frowned. "If you liked it, why have you brought it here?"

This was a highly embarrassing situation, mainly because us thirty-somethings had been close friends for ten years – but would we still be friends after this evening?

"The thing is, Emma," Ros stammered. "The material of the blouse is practically see-through. It became a pain, hunting around for a vest to wear underneath."

"Oh. I wondered why I've never seen you wearing it," I remarked, and scrambled through the heap to pull out a t-shirt with light blue stripes. "This is a better option."

Ros chuckled. "I passed that on to you at my summer barbecue. You'd turned up in a long, floaty dress…"

"This one?" I picked out a familiar frock, patterned with tiny red poppies.

She gasped. "Yes! You didn't like ➡

the dress, so you gave it to me," Ros said. "Anyway, back to the poppy affair. You kept tripping over the hem, so you asked me if I had anything you could borrow. I had a blue stripy t-shirt and a pair of shorts. You were eternally grateful. In fact, you went home in that ensemble."

"Yes, I remember. And here are the shorts we wore with the t-shirt." I selected a pair of khaki baggy horrors.

conversation. However, Ros quickly took charge of the situation…

"Right. Item number one. A gold see-through blouse. Neither of us wants it…"

Someone shouted: "I'll have it!"

Ros chucked it in the caller's direction.

Taking Ros's cue, I picked up the t-shirt. "Item number two. A t-shirt with faded blue stripes. It's a no from me."

"A no from me too," Ros said.

An awkward moment of tension fell between us and we looked sheepish

Ros was baffled. "I didn't expect to ever see them again!"

"I'm mortified. Look, Ros… I'll confess that I didn't realise I'd be seeing you here," I admitted.

"Well, I didn't expect to see you here, either. To be honest, I can understand why you didn't take to the shorts, but why have you brought the t-shirt along? What was wrong with it?"

Under her gaze, I squirmed. "After around fifty washes, the stripes faded. It's why the stripes are light blue, instead of dark. I sort of went off it then."

"I see," she mused.

Then a thought occurred to me. "So why did you bring the poppy print dress?"

"I took the hem up, but when I tried it on, it didn't hang right. Sewing the hem was a mistake – it altered the line of the dress."

An awkward moment of tension fell. We each had very good reasons to try to hide our sheepish faces.

To make matters worse, it was at this moment that we realised everyone had been listening intently to our

"A yes from me!" A voice rang out – and I handed it over.

It was Ros's turn. "Item number three. A floaty poppy print dress with a hand-sewn hem. It may need work. This doesn't get my vote."

"It doesn't get mine either," I muttered.

"It gets mine!" A hand grabbed it.

"Item number four…" I went on. "A pair of khaki shorts. I wouldn't give them house room."

"Nor me," Ros mumbled.

"There's room for them in my house!" Another clothes swapper eagerly scooped them up.

Some might be offended that we brought our swapped garments to a clothes swap party," Ros commented later, as we chilled out with a glass of wine and a plate of tasty treats.

"Well, as soon as I saw you here, I guessed it might happen," I put in.

"It's quite funny when you think about it really, isn't it?" Ros grinned.

We looked at each other for a moment, then burst into giggles, and laughed until the tears ran. MW

Salted Caramel Shortbreads

Ingredients (Makes 20 fingers)
For the shortbread:
- **175g butter, softened**
- **75g caster sugar**
- **250g plain flour**
- **Few drops vanilla essence**

For the caramel:
- **397g can condensed milk**
- **3tbsp golden syrup**
- **150g unsalted butter**
- **1tsp sea salt**

To finish:
- **250g plain chocolate, broken into pieces**
- **50g white chocolate, broken into pieces**

320 calories per square

1 Preheat the oven to 180°C, Fan 160°C, Gas 4. Grease and line a 17x27cm tray bake tin. Place the butter, sugar, flour and vanilla in a bowl and rub together to make a rough dough, or mix in a food processor. Press the mix over the base of the tin and bake for 20-25min. Leave to cool in the tin.

2 Meanwhile make the salted caramel. Place the condensed milk, syrup, butter and sea salt in a heavy based saucepan and stir over a medium heat. Boil for about 10min, stirring to ensure the mix doesn't burn. When it is a deep golden colour, pour on to the shortbread and leave to set.

3 To finish melt the plain chocolate in a heatproof bowl over a saucepan of hot water. Repeat with the white chocolate. Pour the plain chocolate over the caramel and drizzle lines of white chocolate across the width of the tin. Using a skewer, pull through the length of the tin to swirl the white chocolate. Leave to set. Cut into fingers or squares.

RECIPES AND FOOD STYLING: JENNIE SHAPTER
PHOTOGRAPHY: JON WHITAKER

Hope Springs Eternal

Was the retirement home the end of the line for Mavis?
Or was something rather special about to happen?

By Lizzie Lane

On entering St Hilda's Retirement Home, Mavis McQueen clocked the door in the corner and knew instantly that it was special.

Georgian green was a perfectly normal colour for a door, but this one smouldered and glowed and billowed outwards like a bed sheet with a good wind behind it.

At close to eighty years of age, Mavis was used to seeing strange things. She'd seen them all her life, and this door had a comfortable familiarity about it – in the same ballpark as flying in a dream or revisiting childhood haunts.

No one else seemed aware of the amazing spectacle. Her daughter-in-law was prattling on about how lovely this

it's blowing in and out just like a pair of bellows."

This time her daughter-in-law Audrey heard her. Her face creased like a deflated beach ball.

"It's unladylike to shout like a fishwife."

Audrey resumed shouting at the porter to be careful with her mother-in-law's luggage. "Or I'll have the cost of any damage taken out of your wages."

Despite her loud voice, the porter looked unperturbed. He wore an earring through his nose and three more in each ear. The ones in his ear were shaped like stars. He espied Mavis looking at him and winked. Mavis winked back.

Knowing neither her presence nor her input would be welcomed by Audrey, Mavis looked over to the door. It was

The porter wore an earring through his nose. He saw her looking and winked

place was and how much "dear Mum" had been looking forward to living here.

The truth was that she'd hated giving up her cottage and her independence, but for some reason, something about St Hilda's had intrigued her.

"That's an unusual door," she said.

No one was listening to her, so Mavis spoke more loudly.

"I said, there's a door in the corner and

still pulsating and its glowing colour was undiminished. She tilted her head back so that she could see up the stairs to where the first landing vanished into the dark wood panelling.

There was something about St Hilda's that reminded her of the house she had shared with her husband David for thirty years. The feel of the old place with its creaking floorboards and ➤

Gwen Freeman was reassuring.

"Don't worry about that, Mrs McQueen. We're quite used to the wandering minds of the elderly."

"She also pretends to be deaf," said Audrey, throwing an accusing glare at Mavis. "I say something to her and she refuses to answer, though there's nothing wrong with her hearing."

"Rest assured we will cope with all her little foibles," returned Gwen Freeman. "Your mother-in-law's room is on the ground floor, much more convenient when one is confined to a wheelchair. We wouldn't want her to be left stranded on an upper floor if the lift ever goes out of action, do we?"

Her laughter was as brittle as thin ice and was echoed by Audrey.

"We certainly would not," she agreed.

"Has she been in a wheelchair for very long?" Gwen asked.

"No. She can use a walking frame – when she wants to."

Audrey's hand rested on her throat – as though her having to push her mother-in-law's wheelchair was likely to lead to a severed throat or at least severe laryngitis.

Mavis felt more and more diminished, upset that she was being ignored, as though she was a cabbage, not a human being at all. So why had she felt so drawn to this place? Perhaps her instinct had finally let her down.

She attempted to smile at other residents as they shuffled past on walking frames or sticks. They looked at her with vague expressions, then looked away as though they weren't seeing her at all.

"We'll do our best to get her back on her feet," said Gwen Freeman. "We have various hobby groups here and little excursions that might encourage her to get more mobile." She gave a little laugh. "Not that we want her to get too

things that went bump in the night had made her flesh tingle with excitement. She wondered whether the new owners would feel its personality as she had, if they would be aware of past generations embedded in the very walls and sensed rather than seen.

A woman with sandy coloured hair, the buttons of her uniform straining over a large bosom, came over to introduce herself. She spoke directly to Audrey, ignoring Mavis completely.

"I'm Gwen Freeman. We met when you came to view. If you have any questions at all…"

Mavis asked her about the door in the corner. Audrey shook her head.

"My mother-in-law has a vivid imagination, I'm afraid."

mobile. We don't want her wandering off by herself. We do outings now and again; the seaside, bingo, a day at local stately homes and such like."

Audrey's smile was strained and the way her painted fingernails were tapping on her designer handbag left Mavis in no doubt that she was itching to leave.

"Is there much paperwork still to do?" asked Audrey, barely concealing the impatience in her voice.

Gwen Freeman smiled in a benign manner. "It shouldn't be too long now. But as I am sure you will understand, we do have to adhere to the rules and regulations of the powers that be. We are quite strictly regulated."

"I quite understand," returned Audrey.

lifetime of having had much more.

A new beginning, said the voice in her head. The voice had been with her since just after David had died. It had a strangely West Indian lilt about it and for the most part, was one she trusted.

What kind of new beginning?

Honey, just be prepared, the voice replied. She thought the advice a bit ambiguous. Perhaps Audrey was right and she was losing her mind, imagining lots of things that weren't really there.

Be prepared.

"I'm not a boy scout," she blurted forgetting that the voice was in her head.

"No one said you were," Audrey snapped impatiently.

A cloud of perfume – Poison, she

The voice in her head had been with her since just after David had died

Mavis's son, Richard, came back with the paperwork.

"All done," he said, smiling down at his mother as he slipped his copies into the shiny St Hilda's folder. "We can now take you to your room, Mother. Your luggage should already be there."

The room allocated to Mavis was in the older part of the house. Its lead-paned windows sparkled like diamonds in the sunlight. A beam ran along the top of the wall at ceiling height, evidence that Mavis's room had been part of a far larger one, now divided into smaller units to cater for the elderly.

A single bed, a chest of drawers, an armchair, a wardrobe and a television, perched on a shelf above another for books and family photographs.

Mavis felt tears pricking the back of her eyes. This was it. She had reached the end of the line; one small room after a

thought it was called – fell over Mavis as Audrey leaned over her to put on the brakes of the wheelchair.

Mavis let her mind wander, recalling other times even before she'd been a wife, a mother, a grandmother and smiled at her memories. Audrey spotted it.

"What's that smile about? In another world again?"

"That's right. My world," Mavis muttered. "It's the only place I feel happy."

Audrey ignored her, too busy dragging the contents out from one of the bags.

"It won't take a moment. I'll have it done in no time. We don't have enough time to deal with the trivialities and believe me I wouldn't offer if it didn't fit in with our schedule. We have a dinner party at seven…"

"As long as there's a wi-fi connection. I need to use my tablet," stated Mavis.

"There is, but do you know how to use it?" Audrey sneered. ➡

"She can," Richard confirmed.

Audrey looked at her husband with considerable surprise.

"Can she indeed? Then I suppose I'd better check."

She flipped open the tablet before Mavis could snatch it from her.

"What's this?"

Her eyes raced over the page Mavis had last saved.

"Who the devil's Troy?"

Richard interceded, taking the tablet gently but firmly from his wife's hands and passing it to his mother.

"I think you'll find it's a place, not a person, dear. Ancient Troy. It was a city the Greeks fought over. I think it's in present day Turkey. It's a very interesting place to visit, so I'm told."

He said it rather hopefully. He'd always nurtured hopes of going on an historical interest holiday.

"Well, if there's no beach, a good sized swimming pool and a buffet breakfast, then I won't be going there," Audrey answered resolutely.

Mavis clutched the tablet to her chest.

"It's my window on the world. It keeps me amused and that's all that matters. I wouldn't have any company if I didn't have that."

"Well, thank you very much! It's nice afraid of upsetting the equilibrium between mother and wife if he didn't tread very carefully?

Mavis sighed. "Please. Just go."

"Come along, Richard! If we're not wanted," Audrey said huffily. "After all we've done, repairing things at Fern Cottage so we could achieve a better price so you wouldn't be destitute."

Mavis gritted her teeth. They'd gained as much for getting the work done as she had, increasing their portion of the proceeds of sale. In his will David had stipulated that their beloved home should be sold and the proceeds divided between his wife and son once she had moved out into more "equitable surroundings".

Once she passed on, everything would go to Richard, which would lead to his wife going on a spending splurge. Probably get the flags out as well.

David, poor love, hadn't expected her to outlive him for too long, and had assumed that moving out would mean going up in a puff of smoke at the crematorium – not tripping over a Labrador and being shifted into a residential home for the elderly.

"Goodbye, then, Mum." Her son kissed her on the cheek.

Audrey did the same, her perfunctory peck dry and sharp.

Blond-haired, long-limbed Troy. First love, like a candle in the wind

to be so appreciated," snapped Audrey.

"You have a social life. I don't," Mavis returned.

Richard looked stung.

"Oh, Mum, please don't take on like that. You make me feel so bad."

She tried to remember when Richard had taken on that whining voice, a sure sign that he was sitting on the fence,

After they'd gone, Mavis sat hugging her tablet to her chest attempting to analyse why she wasn't crying, why her feelings were so mixed.

She'd been a strong, independent woman all her life, outspoken and sometimes a bit wild. Just because she was old didn't mean anything had changed. She was still Mavis Nash who became Mrs Mavis McQueen, a woman who saw things other people didn't see and healthily accepted that it takes all sorts to make a world.

She quite often reminisced about her life, how it had been lived, the fun, the laughter, the tears and the pain. Despite everything, life to her had tasted as sweet as wine.

Get a grip, Mavis. It ain't over yet!

"Truth is I'd relish tasting it all over again," she whispered in response to the voice in her head.

She sighed. Surely there were other seniors who felt the same? Or perhaps she really was becoming senile?

She contemplated the sad fact that she'd not appreciated her youth while she'd had it. Each decision made had mapped out the path of her life, but what if she'd made a different decision and gone down a different path? Where might that have led her?

She thought of Troy. She'd loved her husband, but whenever friction arose between them her thoughts had returned to the blond-haired, long-limbed Troy. First love, like a candle in the wind, an itch she'd never been able to scratch. That candle had been extinguished a long time ago but sometimes, just sometimes, it flickered into life.

Hey! He was the one, huh?

"He was the one."

But what if?

That voice in her head again.

"Only two letters, but if is a big word," she said solemnly.

She was still sitting there when a staff member came to take her into dinner.

"Everyone is waiting to meet you," he said, his smile as bright as sunshine and his eyes sparkling as though party to a secret that as yet she was not.

She thought of the people with the vague eyes and her heart sank.

Heads turned as she was wheeled into the dining room. The room was magnificent and dominated by a huge fireplace. Paintings of women in long dresses and men in doublet and hose or long cloaks looked down at her.

The residents were all smiling at her, that same look as the carer who had wheeled her into the room. Were these really the same people she'd seen earlier.

One face above all others caught her attention and her jaw dropped.

"Mavis? Remember me? It's Troy."

She would have recognised him anywhere even though his thick mane of hair was no longer blond but white, his jaw only a little softer. The only obvious sign of age was his stiffness when he got to his feet.

His smile took her back to the years of their youth. He took hold of her hands and raised her gently but firmly from the wheelchair, his eyes boring into hers. ➤

"We like to put relatives' minds at rest, to believe this is a home like any other"

"I knew you'd understand the message and get here eventually. I remembered your second sight – and once you became a widow…"

*The best is yet to come…*The words popped into her head, though stronger than they'd ever been before.

Out of the corner of her eye she saw a tall man of Caribbean heritage, his hair snowy white, a glint in his smiling eyes.

"Errol's been in constant touch with you for a while now," Troy explained, nodding to him with a smile.

Mavis shook her head.

"Am I dreaming? This all seems so unreal. What is this place?"

Troy led her to a dining chair. The table was laid with crisp white linen and sparkling silverware.

He remained holding her hands as she sat down, and smiled down gently into her face.

"You see, Mavis, living here is by invitation only. I take it you've seen the door?"

She nodded. "Yes." Her voice was small and full of wonder.

"It's the door to the past. Step through it and you live a chosen moment all over again until you no longer have need of the past, until you accept that we

are all made of stars and to stars we shall return. Until then…" He leaned forward and kissed her cheek. "Enjoy the time you have left. Revisit the past as long as you need to."

"What about the staff here?" She recalled Gwen Freeman and the way she'd talked over her to Audrey.

Troy smiled. "We like to put the relatives' minds at rest, to have them believe that this is a retirement home no different than any other."

She thought of Audrey and her impatience to have her out from under her feet, and began to laugh.

"I'm so glad she won't be visiting too often. I won't know what to say."

"You'll get used to putting on an act," said Troy. "Just don't overdo the sympathy card or they might believe you and take you away from here."

Before going to bed that evening and hand in hand with Troy, she and a few other residents eyed the door beneath the stairs. It was still pulsing bright green, inviting her and the others to enter whenever they wanted. Her old life was over, replaced by something different, a bridge between the past and the future. The best was yet to come, undoubtedly. MW

Brain Boosters

Sudoku

			6		4			
5				1				2
	3	1						6
7		9	3	5				4
		2				3		
3				1	4	6		7
4						2	1	
1			4					5
	2			9				

Fill in each of the blank squares with the numbers 1 to 9, so that each row, each column and each 3x3 cell contains all the numbers from 1 to 9.

Word Wheel

Turn To P171-173 For Solutions

You have ten minutes to find as many words as possible using the letters in the wheel. Each word must be three letters or more and contain the central letter. Use each letter once and no plurals, foreign words or proper nouns are allowed. There is at least one nine-letter word.

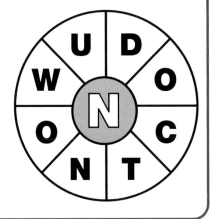

Average: 15 words
Good: 16-22 words
Excellent: 23-29 words

Too Many Crooks

The house next door was empty, so she felt duty bound to investigate what was going bump in the night...

By Lin Silver

Sara woke with a start. Thump, thump – a steady noise like footsteps coming from next door, the house that had been empty for almost a year! She scrambled out of bed and hurried downstairs, pulled on her coat and grabbed the key to next door.

Old Mrs Barrett had trusted Sara with her spare key "just in case" because of her forgetfulness. Fortunately Sara had never needed to use it and had almost forgotten she still had it, until now. She peered over the fence. There were no lights on, although it was reasonable to assume the electricity had been cut off months ago.

Sara hesitated. Should she go in? Curiosity got the better of her and she opened the front door.

sound, coming from somewhere at the back of the kitchen. Common sense suggested surely it could be no more than an animal who had found its way in and now couldn't get out.

She walked cautiously towards the kitchen. She felt the cold breeze before she was able to make out that the back door was open and swinging slightly on its hinges.

"Is anyone there?" she called out.

She wasn't sure, but thought she heard muffled whispering from somewhere. Then a loud, grating sound almost made her jump out of her skin.

With it came a blast of cold air, and when she summoned enough courage to take a look, she saw the old sash window in the living room was open. Now she knew for certain that it was time to call

She didn't believe in ghosts, but it was all getting a bit creepy now

She heard a rustling sound from somewhere and froze. The place was full of cobwebs and pitch black, except for the light from the streetlamp outside. The noise continued.

"Hello?" she called.

Silence. Sara didn't believe in ghosts, but it was all getting a bit creepy now. And at that moment, she heard a rattling

the police. She extracted her phone from her coat pocket and quickly dialled the emergency number.

"Police, please," she said, quietly.

"No, don't worry! They're already on their way!" bellowed a man's voice from somewhere in the dark.

"And I called them!" came a younger voice from the gloomy recesses. ➤

"But Joan called them!" shouted someone else from upstairs.

Sara was bewildered. She leaned against the dusty wall and wished for all the world there was more light.

Seconds later, the place lit up like a Christmas tree as not one, but two police cars pulled up outside and four burly police officers barged into the late Mrs

"And me, but I couldn't find mine so I climbed through the window," admitted young Jacob from number fourteen.

It quickly became obvious to Sara that one of the things the old lady had forgotten was how many of her neighbours she'd given a spare key to!

"Any point in asking why you are all here?" one of the other officers asked.

"Under arrest? But, officer, I'm the one who just called you here..."

Barrett's crumbling house.

"Stay where you are, you're under arrest!" one of them barked.

Sara froze, but elsewhere there was sudden hectic movement as people emerged from the shadows and all began speaking at once.

"But I'm the one that called you!"

"So did I, I called you!"

"No, it was me!"

Sara didn't bother adding that she too had also been in the process of calling the law. In the bright, blinding light from the officer's torches, she could now see a selection of her other neighbours trooping down the stairs, out of the kitchen, and from the dank living room. Everyone was in their nightclothes, like herself, with just a coat or dressing gown hastily thrown over the top.

"So none of you broke in?" the officer asked, looking bemused. Or rather, amused.

"No!" came the unified response.

"Mary Barrett gave me a spare key, in case she ever locked herself out."

"She gave us one, too!"

Answers came fast and furious.

"I heard a noise!"

"I saw the gate swing!"

"There was thumping!"

"Oh, sorry, that was me."

Everyone fell silent and turned to stare at a man who'd suddenly walked in through the back door.

"I came back to try and find my dog's favourite toy – he's going mad because it's missing," the stranger explained. "We were out walking earlier, he wormed his way in here, and out again very quickly, but minus that wretched toy! No one can sleep back home for the noise he's making, howling and barking!"

Silence. Then everyone started laughing.

"Nice to know people are so conscientious round here!" said one of the police.

Sara turned to the culprit.

"But the question is, have you found your dog's toy?"

The man smiled and held up a well-chewed rubber bone.

"Well," Sara concluded, laughing. "In the light of that evidence, I'd say, case closed!" MW

Curried Chicken Pizza Grills

547 calories per square

Ingredients (Serves 2)

- **2tsp vegetable oil**
- **1 onion, peeled and thinly sliced**
- **2tsp medium curry powder**
- **125g cooked chicken, chopped**
- **125g frozen peppers**
- **2 x 120g naan bread**
- **100g plain passata**
- **250g pack reduced fat mozzarella cheese, drained and cut into pieces**

1 Heat the oil in a saucepan and stir fry the onion for 2min. Reduce the heat to low, add the curry powder, cover with the lid and cook gently for 5min to soften.

2 Stir in the chicken and peppers, re-cover and cook gently for a further 5min until hot. Keep warm.

3 Preheat the grill to medium hot. Arrange the naans on the grill rack, sprinkle with a little water and toast for 1-2min on each side.

4 Spread with passata and top with the chicken mixture and cheese. Grill for a further 3-4min to melt the cheese. Serve immediately, sprinkled with fresh coriander, accompanied with mango chutney.

RECIPES AND FOOD STYLING KATHRYN HAWKINS
PHOTOGRAPHY STUART MACGREGOR

Igniting The Spark

Did I need to worry about my dad suddenly spending so much time in his man cave, rather than with Mum?

By S. Bee

"How's Dad liking his new shed?" I asked, as Mum and I settled on the sofa with a cuppa.

"He's in his element." Mum chuckled.

I nodded. Since retiring five years ago, Dad had hankered after a garden, but as they'd lived in a first floor flat with a communal lawn, it hadn't been possible to plant anything.

So they'd decided to find a bungalow with a garden.

They were lucky, and had stumbled across this one in a local, good area. The landlord was pleased to have mature tenants and the neighbours were nice, too.

When they'd moved in two months ago, Dad had rushed out and bought gardening tools, then designed a colour coded floral plan.

Mum dreamed of a little veg patch, but Dad said there wasn't room for one. Mum was disappointed, yet understood.

Curious, after our cuppa I stepped out to the rather scruffy, bare garden (the colour-coded plan seemed to have been put aside) and rapped on the shed door.

Dad answered with a smile.

"Hello, Sarah love. Fancy a cuppa?" He waved a Thermos flask.

"I've already had one, thanks."

I realised Mum hadn't made a brew for Dad. Well, I reasoned, if he has his Thermos…

I took in an ancient armchair with a cushion, a rug, a newspaper, his radio, and a soft light on the wall. I presumed the radio and light were battery powered.

"This looks cosy," I said.

"It's good to have a man cave. I can escape from your Mum's nattering and listen to my sports station."

I nodded again. Yes, Mum had disliked the radio sport and had nattered about it.

In their flat, Dad had slunk off to the bedroom to listen, wearing headphones, while Mum watched her daytime TV.

"He's like a child out playing. I have to call him in for his meals"

Then he ordered a shed.

"Although it's nice to have him out from under my feet, he's out in the shed for hours," Mum went on. "He's like a child out playing. I call him in for meals."

"It must get cold though," I remarked.

"I layer up, and I wear two pair of socks. But I'd like to install some sort of heating in here," he mused.

"Right." I wondered why, when they

had a perfectly good central heating system inside the house.

This shed is like Dad's second home. Mum has to call him in for meals," I began, as my hubby, Joe and I tucked into our own evening meal later that day.

"Well, he's always wanted a garden, hasn't he?" Joe said.

"But he isn't getting any gardening done. He spends most of his time there reading the paper, drinking tea and listening to the radio."

Joe grinned. "You know what? I don't blame him. And I bet your mum relishes having the TV to herself."

"Yes, but –"

"Chill out, Sarah. Even the most devoted of couples need a bit of 'me' time away from each other, every now and ➡

again," he pointed out reasonably.

"Hmm, I guess so."

Talking of 'me' time… due to company budget cuts, my full-time admin job had recently been reduced to part-time.

We were OK financially, yet once I'd whizzed through the housework, my spare hours at home hung heavy. Hence the visits to my folks.

"I still think they need something they can share. A hobby or a pet."

they peeled off their coats.

"Oh!" I was taken aback.

"We've had our names down with the council for years," Mum explained. "Finally, we've been offered a plot. I can have my veg patch!"

"That's great news," Joe beamed.

"It's given me the motivation to start on the garden," Dad added.

"Your dad and I had a good talk, and realised were both stressed out and tired

"Keep it subtle. You don't want them to think you're meddling in their marriage"

"A pet would keep you company while I'm at work," Joe put in.

We invited my folks to Sunday lunch to voice my suggestion. Joe agreed with me that an allotment offered the ideal solution.

"Keep it subtle," Joe warned. "You don't want them to think you're meddling in their marriage."

Oh dear. Was I meddling in their marriage? I hoped not.

To my surprise, they arrived in an upbeat mood.

"We've got an allotment!" Dad announced, as

with moving," Mum went on. "We needed time to adjust."

That explained why Dad's initial garden enthusiasm had waned.

My heart warmed.

"I'm glad you've reignited your spark."

"Well Sarah, we're going to be quite busy. So your Mum and I have come up with a suggestion. Don't think we're meddling, but now you've got more time on your hands and won't be visiting us so much, how about getting a dog? You'd get out and about, and you'd meet other dog walkers, too."

I smiled.

"What a good idea!" Ⓜ

Brain Boosters

Kriss Kross

Try to fit all the listed words back into the grid.

Turn To
P171-173 For
Solutions

4 letters
SODA
SOUL
7 letters
ADJUDGE
LEOTARD

8 letters
EXEMPLAR
GARGOYLE
MAGNETIC
9 letters
DEMARCATE
MACADAMIA

10 letters
BUDGERIGAR
CLAVICHORD
RABBINICAL

11 letters
CHEERLEADER
GRANDMASTER
GUTTERSNIPE

The Truth About Cats And Dogs

What is Paul letting himself in for, agreeing to look after the pampered Princess for ten days?

By Linda Lewis

Princess is in the kitchen. Make yourself comfy and I'll let her in."

Paul managed a small smile. It wasn't that he didn't like cats, but he was more of a dog person.

As he waited for the animal to appear, every muscle in his body was taut. If things went the way they usually did, the cat would make a beeline for him.

True to form, Princess ran straight to him. After rubbing her head against his leg, she stepped back, then with a graceful leap, landed on his lap.

"She's hoping you'll stroke her," his nephew's face because she chuckled.

"I know. I haven't been away on holiday since Bert popped his clogs, but it's been three years now. It was my friend Enid who talked me into it. What's the point of sitting on a nest egg, she said, when nothing's going to hatch?" She fixed her bright eyes on his. "I was hoping you could take care of Princess for me."

"Can't one of your neighbours do it?"

"Sadly, no. Either they're allergic, or they have dogs."

He tried to think of another candidate.

"I wouldn't ask, but there's no other option. She wouldn't be any trouble. She doesn't go out, she's completely house

She definitely deserved a break. There was no way he could let her down

aunt said, unhelpfully. "Behind the ears is her favourite spot."

Dutifully Paul did as he was told.

When Princess began to purr, Aunt Phyllis smiled warmly.

"I'm so glad she likes you. You see, I'm going to the Isle of Wight next month."

She must have seen the surprise on her

trained. You wouldn't need to come round at lunchtimes – unless you wanted to, of course." She paused and gave the cat a warm and indulgent smile. "She's a fussy eater, but that's just her way."

Paul didn't know what to say. His aunt had been like a mother to him since his parents emigrated to Spain.

"How long are you going for?" he asked, praying for an answer that included the word *weekend*.

"Ten days. We leave on the twelfth of next month." She paused. "You will do this for me, won't you, Paul? It would mean so much to me."

She'd been so good to him. When his last relationship ended, she was there with a hug and homemade cake. And she definitely deserved a break. There was no way he could let her down.

He added the dates to his calendar.

"There, it's in my diary. I'll pick her up the day before. After work."

"Thank you so much." His aunt handed him a flyer. "Have this. In case you have any problems."

He read the details. "*Jasmine Simons. Cats Are Us. More than just a cattery*."

"It's not far from you," Aunt Phyllis added. "I hear she's very good."

Paul clutched at the passing straw.

"Couldn't Princess stay there?"

Aunt Phyllis gasped in dismay.

"Good heavens, no. The poor ➡

darling will think I've abandoned her. It's just in case you have problems, it might help to have someone on hand. Jasmine's lovely. Never married. You'd like her."

Paul smiled.

"Is this more of your matchmaking, Aunty Phyllis?"

The old lady chuckled and shook her head. "Of course not." She stood up. "Now that's settled, I'll put the kettle on. There's some of that homemade fruit cake with cherries in that you like."

As she headed for the kitchen, Paul sighed. He could never say no to his aunt, a fact she knew only too well. Thank goodness she wasn't going on a round-the-world cruise.

Later, as he drove home, he wondered how he'd cope with Princess. It was the way a cat looked at you. It always made him feel like a defenceless mouse.

When his route took him past the cattery, he stopped outside. It might be an idea to introduce himself in case he needed help later on.

Seconds after he rang the bell, a woman appeared. Her eyes were a striking shade of green, just like Princess's.

"Are you Jasmine Simons?"

She nodded, smiling.

"What can I do for you today?"

"I've been asked to look after my aunt's cat while she's on holiday."

Jasmine smiled.

"And you're worried how you'll cope, because you're not a cat person."

"That's about it, yes," he replied, wondering how she could tell.

She pushed a flyer towards him.

"You need this." She tapped the page. *How to get on with your cat,* it read.

The cost was thirty pounds.

Paul gulped. "That seems like quite a lot of money."

Jasmine lowered her voice so that it sounded more like a husky purr.

"If your aunt enjoys her holiday, you might end up cat sitting, three, maybe four times a year."

Paul had wondered about that himself but it was having the opportunity to spend more time with Jasmine that decided him. He pulled out his debit card.

On Saturday morning, Jasmine came to his house. As she settled onto his sofa, she seemed completely at ease. Everything she did signalled confidence, grace and elegance.

She took out her tablet.

"First, you need to tell me why you don't like cats. Are you allergic to them?"

"It's nothing like that. It's not that I don't like them, either. They just make me feel… uncomfortable."

"And dogs don't?"

Paul shook his head.

phone number's on the back, there, too."

"Thanks."

After she'd gone, he sat in the living room for ages, breathing in her scent until the phone rang. It was his aunt.

"How did you get on at the cattery?"

He hadn't told her he was going to

"When a cat walks into a room full of cat lovers, what does it do?" she asked

"Dogs are easier. You throw a ball, or give them a treat, and then you're best friends. With cats, I can't relax. I feel I'm being watched."

"That's because you are," she said softly. "When a cat walks into a room full of cat lovers, they all lean forward, but what does the cat do? It heads for one the person who doesn't like cats." She paused. "Why do you think that is, Paul?

He laughed. "I have no idea."

"Cats don't like being stared at. They find it aggressive. So they make for the person who isn't looking at them. " She stood up. "Now the fun part – a demonstration. I'll be right back."

Two minutes later, she reappeared with a large white cat tucked under her arm.

"This is Pugsy. He's staying with us while his owner tours the USA." She put the cat on the floor. "Lean forward. Try to make eye contact with him."

When the cat sat down and started grooming itself, completely ignoring him, Paul was amazed.

"Let me get you a coffee," he offered.

When he came back with the drinks, the cat was on Jasmine's lap, purring.

"When do you collect Princess?" she asked, scratching Pugsy's jaw.

"Next Friday. "

She nodded.

"If you need any help, give me a call." She handed him her card. "My personal

drop in. Sometimes Paul wondered if his aunt could read minds.

"Jasmine came round this morning. She was very helpful."

"Great. So you're still good to go?"

"Yes. I'm looking forward to it," Paul replied and realised that he meant it.

Inspired by Jasmine, he spent an hour online that night, finding out more about cat behaviour. It was fascinating.

As he read, so many things began to make sense. When the time came to collect Princess, his anxiety had vanished.

Princess settled in and behaved perfectly, only climbing onto to his lap when he gave the right signals. His research revealed that cats preferred their food served at room temperature, rather than straight from the fridge. That and offering smaller portions cured her fussy eating problem.

After three days, it was though he'd always had a cat. Whenever he could, he popped home at lunchtime. It was nice to always get a warm welcome.

The days had flown by. He'd been getting along with Princess so well, he'd had no reason to call Jasmine. He was running out of time.

Princess purred, making him chuckle.

"You're right. Faint heart never won fair lady. If she says no, I'm no worse off than I am now, am I?" ➜

Even as he reached for the phone, it started ringing.

"Hi, it's Jasmine. I called to see how you were getting along with Princess. It's just that I'll be passing your door in a minute or two. If there's anything at all, I'd be happy to pop in."

Paul smiled.

"Now you mention it, there is something I'd like to discuss with you."

"Good. I'll be there in five."

It seemed like only seconds before she was there, looking at him expectantly. Paul swallowed as she settled on his sofa, long legs elegantly crossed at the ankle.

"Would you like to go out to dinner with me sometime?"

Over coffee, two mugs each, she showed him hundreds of photos on her phone. After she'd gone, Paul sat grinning like a fool. Jasmine really was an amazing woman. He couldn't wait to see her again.

When his aunt came to collect Princess, relaxed and cheery from her break, she asked how they had got on.

"Absolutely fine. I've fixed her fussy eating, too." He told his aunt what he'd found out online.

"Well I never," replied Aunt Phyllis. "That's wonderful, because I've booked another holiday. Next month, I'm going on a canal boat with a lovely man I met on the Isle of Wight. You'll be OK having Princess again, will you?"

"Hmm, let me guess. There's something you're not telling me, isn't there?"

Jasmine shook her head regretfully.

"Actually I don't enjoy eating out. Restaurant food's never as good as I can have at home."

Having taken the plunge, Paul wasn't ready to give up.

"How about the cinema instead?"

Jasmine grinned. "That sounds great. I could make us something to eat before we went. Do you like lamb? Good." Jasmine scribbled a note and handed it to him. "That's my address. I'll see you seven o'clock sharp on Friday."

As she got up to leave, Paul had a question. "Just so I'm prepared, exactly how many cats do you have?"

She laughed. "I don't have any."

"Sorry? What? But I thought you were a cat person, through and through."

"I work with cats but I relax with dogs. I have three, all big and soft as butter. Would you like to see some photos?"

"I would. I'll put the kettle on."

Paul smiled. His aunt would never cease to amaze him.

"It will be my pleasure," he replied.

"Good." She gave him a hug. "So how's it going with Jasmine?"

"Very well. We're going to the pictures on Friday." He paused. "Hold on. What makes you think I've seen her?"

His aunt waved a hand in the air.

"I'd recognise her perfume anywhere."

The pieces of the puzzle fell into place.

"Hmm, let me guess. There's something you're not telling me, isn't there?"

Aunt Phyllis held up her hands in mock surrender. "You got me. I went to the cattery, intending to book Princess in, but when I met Jasmine, I knew you'd get on." She paused. "I was right, wasn't I?"

"Yes. As always."

Paul smiled. Once again his aunt had played him like an old violin, but this time he didn't mind at all. MW

Champagne & Raspberry Delights

Ingredients (Serves 2)

- ◆ **2tsp powdered gelatine**
- ◆ **25g caster sugar**
- ◆ **400ml pink champagne or pink sparkling wine**
- ◆ **75g fresh raspberries**

For the heart shortbreads:

- ◆ **30g butter**
- ◆ **15g caster sugar + extra for dusting**
- ◆ **Few drops vanilla essence**
- ◆ **50g plain flour**

1 Place the gelatine in a small saucepan with 4tbsp water. Leave for 5min then add the sugar and heat gently to dissolve the sugar and gelatine. Remove from the heat, slowly stir in the champagne or sparkling wine and transfer to a jug.

2 Place 3 raspberries at the base of two stemmed wine glasses. Pour a little jelly over and chill until starting to set. Repeat with 3 more raspberries and a layer of jelly mix. Chill again until set. Repeat once more with the remaining raspberries and jelly. Chill for 2-3 hours.

3 Meanwhile make the biscuits. Cream the butter and sugar together and mix in the vanilla essence. Gradually knead in the flour to form a dough. Cover with clingfilm and chill for 30mins.

4 Preheat the oven to 180C, Fan 160C, Gas 4. Roll out on a lightly floured surface to about 2.5cm thickness and cut out heart shapes using 5cm and 3.5cm cutters. Place on a baking sheet and bake for 15min or until light golden. Sprinkle with caster sugar and transfer to a wire rack to cool. Serve the champagne and jellies with the heart shortbreads.

RECIPES AND FOOD STYLING JENNIE SHAPTER
PHOTOGRAPHY: JON WHITAKER

The Short Straw

Annabel was a clear winner in the school harvest contest – but she had also won something much more important!

By Lin Silver

Annabel, or, "Miss Watson", knew she was going to be given the most difficult task on her first day back at school the minute she saw Claudia Phillips was in charge.

There had been a grudge between herself and the Head Teacher that had started at Easter when Annabel won the Egg Decorating prize with her team, and was obviously continuing now on the first day of term for the new school year.

"Miss Watson, you and your team will be making a scarecrow," Claudia announced haughtily.

Annabel sighed. She might have known. Everyone else was getting the easy stuff, like a basket of groceries or collections of fallen leaves. Clearly, Claudia wanted to get her own back for Annabel beating her in the Easter Egg contest. It wasn't her fault she'd gone to art college and Claudia hadn't.

"Miss, a scarecrow – how do you make a scarecrow?" her Yellow Team clamoured, obviously intimidated by the challenge. Annabel pinned on a smile and spoke soothingly to the little group of eight-to-nine-year-olds in her charge.

"Oh, it's easy!" she assured them, wishing she could assure herself like that. "When you go home today, see what you can find to help make a really good scarecrow. Like, for instance – an old hat, or a mackintosh…"

The children looked blank and puzzled since old hats and mackintosh's didn't exist in their day and age. Annabel could almost feel Claudia gloating.

"Alright, leave it to me – I'll bring in everything we need," she said, praying there'd be some miracle and she would be able to. "We'll win the Harvest Festival Competition, won't we?"

"Yes, yes! We'll beat the Greens!" cried the kids.

"And the Reds," Annabel murmured, with a sly smirk in Claudia's direction. How she would actually make that a

"How do you make a scarecrow?" her team had cried, intimidated by the task

reality, was a bit of a mystery. Claudia and her Red Team had a far easier task.

The first day back was never too tiring, so Annabel didn't feel exhausted when she got home and found her sister and nephew Thomas there.

"Oh, sorry sis, could you look after

him for a bit while I go to the dentist's?" Lorrie babbled. "I've already cancelled this appointment twice, they'll take me off their books if I do it again. I know I should've phoned but I don't like disturbing you when you're at work."

Annabel chuckled softly.

"It would be OK, you know, I'm not working for the government or something," she smiled.

"No, but… anyway, can I leave him with you? He wants to go for a walk. And don't let him paddle in the dirty ditch-water – it's dirty!"

"Yay! Dirty ditch-water! Full of slimy snails!" Thomas cheered, right on cue, a typical boy, if ever there was one. Annabel felt her affection towards him swell.

"Well, we'll look at it, but we won't go in it," she cautioned Thomas,

while his mum was still hovering.

"I'll be about an hour – two at most," Lorrie said as she headed out the door.

"Well, Thomas – we'd better set off on our expedition, hadn't we?" Annabel said brightly to the eager five-year-old.

Thomas loved these walks down the lane and Annabel loved taking him. He showed signs of being a future naturalist, unlike her sister who preferred shops and offices to this rural area. She'd moved away as soon as she'd met Barry and got a job in town, whereas Annabel had been

happy to stay in the house they'd been born and brought up in.

"How was your first day at school, Tom?" Annabel asked, as they set off.

"It was great. They've got fish!" Thomas told her proudly.

Annabel smiled, aware that the infants' school he'd started at liked to spearhead nature projects. At least Barry and Lorrie had had the sense not to send him to some highly academically acclaimed establishment.

Until that point, she'd forgotten her ➡

own school dilemma with the scarecrow-making task.

Thomas's next remark swiftly reminded her. "Can we see Scarecrow Joe?" he asked.

Scarecrow Joe. Created by a farmer, named by Annabel. Thomas always loved to see the rickety old figure stuck in the middle of the cornfield opposite the church. His fertile imagination led him to believe the scarecrow came alive at night and tried to eat all the birds that dared come near him.

"Of course we can," Annabel said, having crossed the narrow road with Thomas many times so he could peep through the fence and believe he saw Scarecrow Joe moving. She often wondered how many of the children in her class would be so delighted with the simple, outdoor things Thomas seemed to love when it was apparent they all came from hi-tech backgrounds. No wonder they'd looked blank about what was needed to make a scarecrow. She could've laughed imagining the unsuitable kind of things they might bring in the next day, were it not for the lingering animosity between herself and Claudia.

They carried on down the lane. Thomas walked fast for

a five-year-old, it was likely he'd be tall, like his dad. They managed to pass the stinging nettles without treading in them this time, then stopped to admire the dirty ditch-Water and dip their fingers in it.

"One, two, three, four five!" Annabel sang softly.

"Once I caught a fish alive!" Thomas sang loudly.

She knew he'd love to catch a real live fish, and she also knew that "Then he'd let it Go Again." She could feel in her bones that her nephew had such a good future with wildlife. Lorrie had probably hoped for a business tycoon, but things always worked out their own way in the end. Anyway, Lorrie had already confided that she and Barry were trying for another…

"Argh! Oh no!"

She was jolted out of her reverie by Thomas's squeal – his school sandal had accidentally slipped into the water.

"Mummy will be cross!" His cute face bore the expression of someone who knew the end of the world was nigh.

"No, Mummy won't have to know," Annabel said, with a secretive smile. "It's

nice and sunny – your sandal will be dried out by the time Mummy comes back."

"But I'll tell her," Thomas said proudly, with his chin stuck out and head held high. "I'll tell her so she knows the dirty ditch-water is safe after all."

Annabel felt a pull at her heart-strings. What a right-minded little soul he was! She hoped that if she ever had kids of her own – and she certainly hoped that

"There he is, there he is! He's being stolen! Stop him, Auntie Anna!"

Annabel could hardly gather her wits quickly enough, but she turned and saw that across the field a man was indeed carrying the uprooted scarecrow away. Obviously it was the farmer, but before she could explain to Thomas, he was shouting out and attracted the man's attention. He stopped, shaded his eyes

Across the field they saw a man who was carrying the uprooted scarecrow away

one day she would – they'd be just like Thomas.

Having dried his sandal with a wad of paper tissues, Annabel and Thomas set off again – heading for the high point of their journey, Scarecrow Joe's field.

However, as they rounded the bend, Thomas emitted another squeal and tugged frantically at Annabel's hand.

"Oh no! He's not there! He's not there! He's gone!"

He was crushed. Annabel thought quickly and came up with something she thought might ease his disappointment.

"Well, this isn't a busy time of year for scarecrows," she said. "With the Harvest, there's not much left in the fields for them to guard. He's probably gone on holiday until the new crops are planted."

"Where d'you think a scarecrow would go on holiday?" Thomas asked, wide-eyed with intense curiosity.

That had Annabel stumped!

"Well – um… probably, a nice dry potting shed," she said eventually, knowing he was far too intelligent to know a scarecrow would not want to go to Brighton or Blackpool!

"Hmm – I s'pose…" Thomas murmured resignedly. Then, suddenly, he was going off like a lit firework again.

and looked, put the scarecrow down and came striding over towards them.

"Don't take Scarecrow Joe! Please don't take him!"

The farmer gave a puzzled little smile, glanced at Annabel but then squatted down to be at Thomas's level.

"So it's Scarecrow Joe, is it?" he said kindly. Thomas nodded, a bit flummoxed by the friendly stranger who now, at close range, could be seen to have bits of loose straw all over his coat and damp patches on his jeans where he'd been kneeling on the ground.

"Well, he's not going anywhere," the man explained in that same amiable tone. "Just in my shed, for the winter. He'll be out again after Christmas, as long as there's no snow on the ground."

"Why, will there be a snowman in his place?" Thomas asked innocently. The man uttered a deep chuckle.

"Well, maybe…" he turned to glance at Annabel, "If your Mum lets you come here to make one!"

"Can I? Can I? She's not my Mum!" Thomas was excited again, looking from one to the other in a frantic manner.

"I'm his auntie," Annabel explained quietly. "Babysitting."

"Oh, but this young man's not ➤

She had that same wonderful feeling Thomas had on first seeing Scarecrow Joe

a baby!" The farmer said determinedly, filling Thomas with pride and delight. "Well, would you like to come and say bye-bye to Scarecrow Joe before he goes into hibernation?"

"What's hibenishon?"

Then, Annabel, Thomas, the farmer and the scarecrow were all walking across the field towards a large shed up by the farmhouse. It looked as though this was proving to be one of the greatest days of Thomas's life.

"There," said the farmer, whose name was Jack, when they reached the shed. "That's Scarecrow Joe safely indoors for winter." A strange prickling sensation suddenly ran down Annabel's spine – and it wasn't just because Jack was about her own age and nice-looking.

"Um, if he won't be needed, is there any chance that I could, um… borrow him for a week?" she asked, hardly daring to breathe. Jack gave her a puzzled smile, so she hastily explained about the school Harvest Contest.

"No problem at all. I could bring him in the truck tomorrow, nice and early," Jack said. Annabel had that same wonderful feeling Thomas must have had upon seeing the scarecrow close up.

"Thank you," she said, feeling that was nowhere near enough.

Scarecrow Joe was already in place when Claudia arrived the following morning. And now he'd been updated a bit with the things the children in Yellow Team had brought in – an iPad, headphones, and a bit of pink colour sprayed on his straw hair. He

easily beat the Greens with their model tractor, the Blues with their food hamper, and the Reds with their model cornfield that looked more like a toy football pitch someone had tried to convert.

Scarecrow Joe was a clear winner and Annabel took a lot of credit for her "intuition". Very unexpectedly, Claudia was one of the first people to congratulate her as she accepted the cheque from the school committee to go towards a better Crafts room.

"You really are very arty," she said. "I'm sorry if I seemed a bit derisive."

"It's fine," Annabel assured her, feeling happier than she had in a long time. Everyone was happy, and best of all, she would meet up with Jack again when he came to pick up Scarecrow Joe. Ⓜ

Brain Boosters

Codeword

Each letter of the alphabet has been replaced by a number. The numbers for the first name of our chosen celebrity are given. Complete the puzzle to reveal which *Corrie* actor Sue Nicholls treats as if he is her real son.

13	3	2	3	22	1	15	5	19	20	12	■	19	5	21
15	■	15	■	15	■	25	■	7	■	3	■	18	■	15
22	5	21	11	3	■	14	20	3	21	7	1	15	16	25
1	■	11	■	19	■	10	■	■	■	7	■	26	■	15
10	17	6	19	18	19	■	6	21	7	10	22	6	3	20
■	■	10	■	■						1	■	25	■	15
14	3	19	26	19						■	3	23	15	23
15	■	■	■	■										5
25	3	23	19	■						20	6	18	22	10
9	■	5	■	4						■	6	■	■	■
5	25	25	10	22	8	10	1	■	24	3	21	21	10	1
10	■	4	■	15	■	■	18	■	20	■	7	■	22	
19	7	6	20	20	15	8	10	22	■	6	25	3	25	10
18	■	22	■	6	■	3	■	6	■	11	■	25	■	3
19	5	10	■	14	15	25	1	15	21	6	25	6	5	21
	S	**U**	**E**											

A B C D É F G H I J K L M N O P Q R Ṣ T Ų V W X Y Z

1	2	3	4	5	6	7	8	9	10	11	12	13
				U					**E**			
14	15	16	17	18	19	20	21	22	23	24	25	26
					S							

Turn To P171-173 For Solutions

24	3	14	26	7	.	19	13	10	7	13	10	22	1
						S		**E**			**E**		

Trial Run

She had thought she wanted a house full of people, so how could she decide if she wanted this job…?

By Patsy Collins

"Thank you for your kind offer to fill in for me, Julia, but that won't be needed after all," Allie said.

Julia tried to match her boss's uncertain smile. "Oh. If you're sure?" Really, Julia hadn't so much offered to cover during her boss's holiday, as constantly begged Allie to increase her hours in the florist shop. Her boss had finally agreed because she wanted a fortnight off in the school holidays and Sally, the only other member of staff, had already arranged to work reduced hours then, to be with her children.

"You're not going to close for the fortnight, are you?" Julia really hoped not. It would be bad for business and leave her with absolutely nothing to do for two whole weeks.

of two weeks of busy usefulness to look forward to. If she'd realised retirement would be so boring, she'd have delayed it a few years.

At the time though she'd looked forward to it – in the same way she'd looked forward to school holidays as a child. At last she'd had the time to renovate the huge seafront house which had been her childhood home.

However, the work was all done now and Julia – fit, healthy and only sixty-three – was bored.

Belatedly Julia realised that if Allie's time off was cancelled then so must be the visit from her family, which Allie had been looking forward to for ages.

"What's happened?" she asked.

"All the local B&Bs and hotels are full for the school holidays, except The Grand and they simply can't afford to stay there."

She didn't miss the rubble and dust and noise, but she did miss the workmen

"No, I'll be coming in. I hope you weren't counting on the extra money?" Allie sounded more concerned than Julia would have expected, despite her boss's kind nature.

"No, that's OK." Julia didn't like to say so, when the others were short of money, but that aspect wasn't a big concern. She only earned minimum wage in the florist shop but she had a good company pension from her old job.

Julia's disappointment was at the loss

"Oh, that's such a shame."

Allie lived in a one bedroomed flat, so was unable to put them up herself.

It wasn't until she returned to her five bedroom home that a solution occurred to Julia. Allie's family could stay with her. She wouldn't accept any money of course. If they offered she'd say she couldn't accept as she wasn't really a bed and breakfast operator… but perhaps, if she enjoyed the experience, she could

become one? Julia mulled over the idea as she made her supper. Why not?

There was clearly a demand for more reasonably priced accommodation in the area and she had all that space going to waste.

Besides, it wasn't much fun living such a predictable routine. To open the fridge and see just what she needed, no more

no less. For the house and everything in it always pristine and exactly as she left it.

For the first couple of years after her retirement the house had been filled with workmen of every description. Julia didn't miss the rubble and dust, nor the whine of power tools, but she missed them. Missed making endless cups of tea and chatting about plans. Those of the work to be ➤

done and what the men, and one woman, would be doing in their free time. She missed having a part in other people's lives. Her one day a week in the florist shop gave her a little of that same feeling, but not enough.

The more she considered it, the better the holiday landlady idea seemed. She had no doubts she could handle the organisational side and cook up hearty breakfasts. Perhaps the cleaning and washing of bedlinen too, but if not she could employ someone for that. There were plenty of small firms offering the service locally; she regularly passed their vans on the way into town. The booking fees would cover the costs and she didn't need to make much of a profit for it to be worthwhile.

Maybe there were drawbacks she hadn't considered?

Having Allie's family to stay would be a novelty and there'd be no pressure on her. However, that wouldn't be enough for a proper trial run. Her own family could provide that. There was six weeks of school holidays, so even if most of them wanted to come, she could fit them all in once Allie's family had left.

As Julia rang to invite her various young cousins to stay, and was rewarded by their eager acceptances, she wondered why she'd never thought to do it before. She'd have liked to see more of them and dropped subtle hints.

It was only after her conversation with Allie that she'd begun to realise that, for those with school-aged children, a week or two in her picturesque seaside town was unaffordable.

Allie's family were no trouble at all. They had tea and toast with her when she had her own breakfast. As she was working full time during their stay and she wasn't charging them, they refused her offer of a cooked meal. They left before Julia set off for the florist shop and were gone until long after her return. There was plenty of time for her to clean the bathrooms and do the small amount of tidying required, despite covering Allie's hours in the shop.

Julia managed to eat quite a lot of the sausages, tomatoes and mushrooms they couldn't be persuaded to let her cook for them and the bacon and eggs would keep until the following week, when she'd have an entire house full.

The first group of Julia's own family were no trouble either. Not really. Their breakfast tastes weren't generally as she'd anticipated, but a quick visit to the supermarket for their favourite cereals and fromage frais put that right, and Julia was developing a taste for sausage sandwiches, so very little was wasted.

But, gosh they were noisy!

Then there was the awkwardness of when to get up in the morning. She didn't want them to feel that they couldn't come down and have a cup of tea until they heard her moving about, but neither did she like to disturb them if they wished to sleep in.

Once she was up, she had to be ready for chatting and cooking. No slowly waking up, sitting in her dressing gown with a quiet cup of tea until she was ready to face the day. That didn't matter though, with so many people to look after, there wasn't time for sitting around. Which was exactly what she'd hoped for.

Plus of course it had been lovely to see them all and really feel part of their lives for a short time.

Then there was a mad scramble to get all the linen washed, dried and back in place before the next batch arrived. The bathrooms needed a lot of attention as she'd only found time for a quick wipe round while they were there. Also, she'd have to get someone in to sort out that recent dent in the plaster board. It would have been an accident of course, but just how had they managed to do that?

Thank goodness that Allie was repaying some of the fortnight Julia had covered for her, by giving her the next four Saturdays off.

"After your generosity and wonderful kindness which allowed me to see my

had to cook them and have her house filled with their grease and cloying smell.

Her family liked to watch television, but talked over it, so she could neither properly concentrate on the programme nor what they were saying. She wanted them to feel at home though, and they did seem to be enjoying themselves.

Half of them were keen cyclists.

"There are loads of brilliant trails all around your area," they'd told her, so of course she'd suggested they bring their machines. They leaned them against painted walls and French windows. It wasn't just the bikes either. Helmets and gloves, maps, backpacks and water bottles, devices for measuring speed and distance were heaped up around them.

Bathrooms were draped in garish advertising-festooned Lycra tops and those awful padded shorts. She wouldn't

There was no slowly waking up, sitting in her dressing gown with a cup of tea

family, it's only fair I let you have as much time as possible with yours."

Accepting had been the only way to cut off yet more effusive thanks.

Julia's next group of family visitors were just as pleasant company and just as appreciative of her efforts on their behalf. Perhaps too much so, as they kept making their own drinks and snacks, putting everything back in the wrong places. Not their fault of course, but it did make preparing breakfast extra stressful.

Learning from past experience, she hadn't bought sausages before enquiring if they liked them.

"Absolutely love 'em," they assured.

After four weeks of eating them almost every day, Julia's enthusiasm was waning, yet because she'd made the offer, she still

have wanted to move them all to clean the showers, even if she'd had the energy.

The others were walkers and despite the hot dry weather, managed to tread quite a bit of mud into Julia's carpets.

She hugged them goodbye with real warmth and said, "I hope you'll be able to come again." She meant it, but perhaps a weekend would be better next time and maybe not all of them at once.

The next morning she'd had her first cup of tea, while still in her dressing gown, and had lost track of time, sitting savouring the peace – and lack of hot sausage fat sizzling in the pan. As a result, for the first time ever she was a little late for work. Allie and Sally were already there when she rushed in, full of apologies and explanations. ➡

"We were talking about families. Hope you enjoyed seeing all yours?" Allie asked.

She could honestly say she'd had a wonderful time during the various visits, due to properly getting to know the

so nice. Being wanted and useful, but able to leave it all behind at the end of the day and return to her lovely quiet house. It was what she'd been asking for these last few months, but would it be as pleasant as

The novelty of playing seaside landlady had long since worn off completely!

youngsters she rarely saw, and to feeling wanted and connected.

"I was wondering if you'd like to go full time?" Allie said.

"Good grief no!" The novelty of playing seaside landlady had long since worn off.

Allie and Sally looked surprised. Astonished even. "You want to stick with just Saturdays, then?"

"Sorry, I misunderstood," Julia said.

"I'm pregnant again," Sally said.

"Congratulations, that's wonderful news! Oh! You're going to give up your job?" She turned to Allie. "And you wondered if I'd like it?"

"Exactly."

Julia thought of nice quiet flowers that stayed where she put them and smelled

she'd imagined? She'd thought she wanted something quite different and been proved wrong. Right now she was filled with enthusiasm at the idea, but would it quickly feel like a dull routine?

"How about I cover your maternity leave as a trial run and see how it goes?"

"Fine with me," Sally said.

"Deal!" said Allie. "Now you said you missed breakfast and Sally is eating for two, so how about I treat us all to something from the cafe to celebrate?"

"Alright, but only if I go and fetch them," Julia said. There was no way she was risking them bringing her a sausage or bacon bap. After the last few weeks, she was off all cooked breakfast foods for the foreseeable future! Ⓜ

Spicy Prawn Tacos With Mango Salsa

170 calories per taco

Ingredients (Serves 4)

- **400g raw king prawns**
- **2tbsp sunflower oil**
- **2tsp ground coriander**
- **2tsp mild chilli powder**
- **Juice 1 lemon**
- **8 corn taco shells**
- **200g red cabbage, shredded**
- **1 carrot, grated**
- **Juice 1 lime**
- **Salt and freshly ground**
- **Black pepper**

For the mango salsa:

- **1 mango, stoned, peeled and chopped**
- **1 red onion, chopped**
- **2tbsp chopped coriander**
- **1 jalapeno pepper, deseeded and chopped**

1 Mix together the ingredients for the mango salsa and set aside. Place the prawns in a bowl. Add 1tbsp oil, coriander, chilli powder and lemon juice and toss together. Season with salt and freshly ground black pepper.

2 Preheat the oven to 160°C, Fan 150°C, Gas 3. Place the taco shells on a baking sheet, open side down and warm for 5mins. Heat the remaining oil in a large frying pan and add the prawns and marinade. Stir-fry for 3mins, or until the prawns turn pink.

3 To assemble the tacos, mix the cabbage, carrot and lime juice together and divide between each shell. Top with the prawns and mango salsa.

No Ghost Unturned

Emily had managed to solve the house's whodunnit mystery – even if the culprits were ghosts…

By Jacqui Cooper

A re you the new tenant?"
Standing on the doorstep, juggling bags and keys, Emily hadn't noticed the man in next door's garden trimming the hedge. He was shirtless, revealing a rather impressive physique, and she struggled not to stare. If this was her new neighbour, things were looking up.

"Yes. I'm Emily. Pleased to meet you."

"Martin." He paused dramatically. "They'll warned you about the ghosts?"

Her smile slipped. "Ghosts?"

"Nobody stays long. That house is haunted, you know."

"I ain't afraid of no ghosts," she sang.

"Eh?"

Who didn't get the *Ghostbusters* reference? "Thanks for the warning but I'm sure I'll be OK," she told him. "Nice meeting you, Martin." She opened the front door and stepped inside only to come face to face with an old woman in a purple housecoat.

"Oh!" said Emily, startled. "I'm so sorry. I must have the wrong –"

"You can see me?" The old woman seemed equally surprised.

How could anyone miss vibrant purple chenille? "I'm really sorry. The agent –"

"And hear me!" The old woman clapped her hands in delight. "You have no idea how long it's been since we've had one like you. Come in, my dear."

"One…one like me?"

"Yes. It is so tiresome living with people who look right through you. Mind you, the ones who can see us don't usually stay long. This is wonderful! Would it be too forward to ask you to leave the telly on when you go out? Is *Crossroads* still on? Oh, would you listen to me! I'm Florence by the way."

"This *is* number twenty eight?" Emily had been here last week with the letting agent. She was pretty sure there hadn't been a woman in a purple housecoat in residence then.

"That's right dear. I lived here from 1972 to 1979," said Florence happily. "Died watching *The Two Ronnies*. I laughed so hard I choked on a digestive." She chuckled. "Not a bad way to go."

Emily blinked. "D… died?"

"Yes dear. Now come along. You look as if you've seen a… never mind. Cup of tea will soon put that right, though you'll have to make it yourself, I'm afraid."

Emily looked round wildly. Where were the cameras? Was this a joke?

A Siamese cat strolled in. "You have a cat." Emily bent to stroke it and her hand passed right through.

"That's Chester. He's a ghost too."

"Of course he is," said Emily weakly.

"Well, well, what have we here?"

She spun to face a tall, brooding

Heathcliff lookalike. His shirt collar was open, his tie tugged loose.

"Andrew, be nice," warned Florence.

Emily hadn't felt any sense of presence from Florence. But Andrew's proximity raised goosebumps on her arms. She shivered, though his dark, smouldering scowl was ruined by the cat rubbing against him, purring madly.

Out of the corner of her eye she noticed a woman at the top of the stairs, wearing only a fluffy pink bath towel.

"Karen," said Florence. "Andrew's

wife. Now you've met everyone."

Emily had been pretty calm up till now, but gradually she felt herself giving in to hysteria. "Who… who are you people? Why are you in my house?"

The ghosts exchanged looks. "Isn't it obvious?" said Florence gently. "We died here and we've been here ever since."

"He killed me!" Karen pointed an accusing finger at Andrew.

Andrew glared. "Still harping on about it?" The air crackled as Andrew vanished. Karen followed a second later. ➜

"K…killed?" said Emily.

Florence sighed. "Those two will be the death of me. Put the kettle on and I'll tell you everything."

While Emily gulped down hot, sweet tea, Florence talked nonstop.

"You already know my story. Andrew and Karen…" She pursed her lips. "They'd been married for five years when he became convinced she was having an affair and killed her in a jealous rage. Then, overcome by guilt, he killed himself. That was in 1961."

"That's awful!" said Emily.

"I know. The next door neighbour couldn't wait to tell me all about it when I moved in. But I liked the house. I was happy here and I'm sure you will be too. Karen and Andrew bicker but there really isn't any harm in them. Well, once you get past the murder, I mean. But they can't hurt you," she added quickly.

"Why didn't I see any of you when I came to view the house?" asked Emily.

"It's difficult to manifest around certain people," said Florence. "We've had folk live here for decades and never see us. The letting agent is like that, his mind is so closed that no one else ever sees us when he's here. Oh I'm so happy you've come! Andrew doesn't say much and all Karen does is moan about dying without her make up on. Trust me, that conversation wears thin over time."

Emily seriously doubted that the ghosts would qualify as a good enough reason to get her deposit back. Besides, she already liked Florence, so she made the decision to stay – for now at least.

She didn't see Karen or Andrew again as she unpacked, though Florence followed her about, chattering away. The old woman looked so disappointed when Emily eventually yawned and announced that she was going to bed, that she offered to leave the TV on and left Florence happily binge-watching Cary Grant films.

Reaching her room she found Chester curled up on her bed. Emily had always wanted a cat, and surely a ghost cat would be less trouble than a real one?

Wrong. Chester's wailing woke her at dawn. He didn't let up until she staggered to her feet. Then he headed out the door, waiting for her to follow. In the kitchen the cat circled and yowled as only a Siamese cat can.

"You have to feed him."

Emily jumped. She hadn't seen Andrew sitting at the table. "He goes through this every morning," Andrew explained. "That banshee wail is probably what gives the house the reputation for being haunted."

"It *is* haunted." Emily pointed out.

Feeling foolish and with Chester growing more and more impatient, Emily pretended to pour food into a pretend bowl. The cat sniffed it, turned up his nose and stalked away.

"You do know what you look like?" Andrew seemed to be fighting a smile.

"I'm trying not to think about it." Making coffee, she joined him at the table.

He inhaled deeply. "I miss coffee."

"You can smell it?"

"No. Just a memory, I suppose."

"So what do ghosts do all day?"

"Me? I brood."

"You're very good at it."

"Thank you." Yes, there it was, a ghost of a smile. It completely transformed him.

She cleared her throat. "So… you killed your wife?"

"I did not!" The air around them

crackled. "Sorry," Andrew seemed upset. "I just… don't remember."

"Well, "said Emily awkwardly. "I'd better get ready for work."

Through the day, work kept her so busy that she didn't dwell too much on what was waiting for her at home. But though she had hated house sharing as a student, Emily found that she enjoyed having the ghosts around. Maybe because no one stole her milk.

Every morning she fed Chester imaginary cat food and she and Andrew did the crossword.

In the evenings she and Florence sat down to watch the soaps. Karen developed an obsession with reality TV, while Andrew devoured anything by David Attenborough. Emily had to use her TV, tablet and laptop to keep everyone happy, but it was nice having company.

How are you getting on with your ghosts?" asked the hot gardener next door as she arrived home one day. Even though it was raining he had his shirt off.

"Fine, thanks."

"Even the evil Andrew?"

did the haunting only start with you two?"

"Guilt," said Karen promptly. "Andrew upset the balance with his anger and refusal to accept what he'd done. So now we're trapped here."

The case was so old, Emily didn't really learn much. The police had found Karen in the bath with a bottle of champagne and two glasses on the side of the bath. They assumed the couple were planning a romantic evening but for reasons unknown Andrew had lost his temper and drowned her before calmly sitting down to eat his tea. After which he had taken an overdose.

Karen read over her shoulder. "See!" She glared at Andrew who had materialised beside them. "You monster!" she howled before she vanished.

Andrew looked longingly at Emily's wine. "I'd offer you a glass," she said with sympathy. "But, you know, you're dead."

"She was cheating on me," said Andrew. "I remember that. I was a wine buyer, you see. I was away a lot." His image began to fizz and crackle.

"Whoa!" said Emily. "Turn it down!"

"Sorry." The crackling stopped. "But I just don't remember killing her," he said

That cat's wail is probably what makes people think the house is haunted

Emily had been about to step into the house. "You know the story?" He nodded. "Tell me," she begged.

"Karen was sweet and pretty. Andrew was jealous and angry. Not much more to say. It was quite a scandal at the time."

As soon as she got inside she Googled the murder.

"Stop that!" Karen appeared behind her. "Let sleeping ghosts lie!"

Emily couldn't. "It's an old house. There must have been other deaths. Why

miserably. "Or myself. I was going to divorce her, but in those days I needed to prove her infidelity."

Emily liked Andrew. The more time she spent with him the harder it was to believe that he was capable of killing anyone. She determined to find out what she could.

It took some digging but eventually she managed to unearth a microfiche copy of an old newspaper report which hinted ➤

that Karen was having an affair with next door's gardener.

Emily was still deep in thought about it when she got home.

Andrew was in the kitchen. "What is it?" he asked, seeing her face.

"The night of the mur – the night Karen died. Tell me everything you remember."

Andrew shrugged. "I'd been to France on a buying trip. I wasn't due back till late but I managed to catch an earlier ferry. Karen was going to her mother's but she said she'd leave something for my dinner."

"Did you go upstairs at any time?"

"No." He sounded more confident. "There was some stew on the stove and I heated it up." He frowned. "I thought I heard a noise and went to the bottom of the stairs but the stew started burning and I rushed back. After I ate it I felt sleepy. When I tried to stand up, I fell."

He glanced down, frowning.

"There was something on the floor. A bottle." Then his eyes widened as he looked at Emily.

"I remember! It was Karen's sleeping pills. What were they doing on the floor?"

Emily was beginning to piece things

accused Karen. "You and your lover had a bath, drank some champagne. No need for secrecy with Andrew away.

"After he left, you lingered in the bath. You weren't in any hurry. You'd already put the sleeping pills in the stew and left the bottle so the police would think it was suicide. And you had your alibi ready as you planned to be out of the house. But Andrew came home early.

"What happened? Did you jump up, slip and bang your head? And of course with Andrew drugged he couldn't help you and you drowned…"

"Wait! You killed me?" roared Andrew. "And all this time you let me think it was the other way around!"

Florence crept into the kitchen, no doubt drawn by the raised voices.

"I was leaving with Martin." Karen tossed her head, unrepentant.

"Martin?" said Andrew.

"Next door's gardener," Emily explained.

She threw open the kitchen window.

"I take it you can't come in?" she asked ghostly Martin who was lurking outside – and still without his shirt on.

The truth has eased his spirit, so they're no longer trapped here in this house

together. What if Karen had known about the divorce? If Andrew could prove she was the guilty party, she stood to lose everything.

"Karen!" she called sharply. "I know you're out there. Come in."

Karen slunk in to the kitchen, clutching her towel. "So what?" she sneered. "He got what he deserved. He was going to ruin everything."

"What's she talking about?" asked Andrew, confused.

Emily ignored him. "You did it," she

"I would have been in like a shot if I could," he said, gazing longingly at Karen. "A tree branch fell on me in '63. I've been stuck in the garden ever since, trying to glimpse my love through the window."

"Oh my!" Florence ogled his manly chest while, Chester jumped onto the windowsill, spitting.

"My darling!" Karen flew across the room and reached through the window to take Martin's hand. Gazing into each other's eyes, they began to fade. In seconds, they were gone.

"What just happened?" asked Emily, stunned almost speechless.

"I… I'm not sure, said Andrew.

"I think maybe the truth has eased Andrew's spirit," ventured Florence. "So Karen and Martin are no longer trapped here."

Chester leapt out of the window and vanished. "Chester too?" said Emily, sadly. She looked at the two remaining ghosts in sudden alarm. "How do you feel?"

Florence tentatively patted herself down. "Fine."

"Andrew?"

He nodded pensively. "I think I'm OK."

Suddenly all three were talking at once.

"She actually got away with murder," said Florence.

"The gardener!" muttered Andrew. "What a cliché."

"Well, I hope there's no lipstick in heaven," giggled Emily. "That would her idea of hell."

"You really think she's going to heaven?" Florence snorted.

Emily cooked dinner for herself and poured a glass of special wine she'd bought on Andrew's recommendation. For a while there was a party atmosphere in the cosy kitchen.

Eventually, though, Emily realised that Andrew had grown quiet. She was terrified to see him beginning to blur round the edges.

"No! You can't go!" she cried out.

Then she glanced at Florence, and to her horror, the old woman melted away before her very eyes, a surprised expression on her face.

"No!" wailed Emily. "This isn't what I meant to happen. I –"

"I'm sorry," whispered Andrew. "I don't think I can stay."

He didn't vanish immediately. Emily mourned Florence but she couldn't bear to waste a single moment of Andrew's company. They talked for hours.

When she could barely keep her eyes open, he followed her upstairs and they lay side by side on her bed.

"Will you still be here when I wake up?" she asked him.

"I don't think so," he admitted. "I can hear them. My family. They've been waiting for me. I couldn't face them before, when I thought I was a killer. But now I'm ready to go."

"Then I'll stay awake. You shouldn't be alone when…"

However, she must have drifted off because when she woke Andrew was gone and the house felt truly empty for the first time since she had moved in.

Emily dressed and went downstairs, telling herself that this was her life now. In the kitchen she looked tearfully to where Chester's bowl should be. Maybe she should get a real cat.

"Finally. You're up," said Florence cheerfully.

Emily jumped. "You didn't go?"

"I thought about it," said the old woman. "But I decided it wasn't for me. Not yet anyway. You don't mind?"

"Of course not!"

"I never had children," said Florence shyly. "Or much family to speak of. If it's OK, I'd like to stay for a bit."

"Great!" Emily smiled

Florence smiled too.

"Do you think you could put the telly on for me before you go to work? I never did find out who shot JR…" Ⓜ

The Wrecker's Secret

That dark night the smuggler rescued a shipwrecked maid and who knew where such a thing might lead them?

By Elie Holmes

Bang-bang-bang! Sarah Tanner woke in an instant as the door of her cabin slammed open.

A wide-eyed passenger appeared in the doorway. "We're all doomed!"

Barely had the words left the woman's lips when she was borne away with a cry as the ship pitched violently, throwing Sarah from her bed.

Feeling sick from the constant motion, Sarah quickly dressed. Fingers curling around the door frame, she fought to keep her footing. She was shocked to see water running along the corridor. Above, she could hear dozens of pairs of feet on the planking of the deck.

Spying the Quartermaster, Sarah called out to him, "Sir, what is happening?"

"We're in the teeth of a gale. Cap'n's fighting to keep us afloat but I fear it's only a matter of time."

"A matter of time…?" she echoed.

"Until we sink. This old hulk ain't making it to the New World."

"You think we are going to sink?"

"Not think, girl, know! The wind is driving us onto the shore where the rocks are waiting to finish the job."

"Surely, there must be a safe harbour close by? We're still following the English coast are we not?"

"Safe harbour?" He spat onto the wooden floor. "The only thing waiting out there is a band of cut-throats and thieves. Wreckers by another name! We're in Cornish waters now, Miss."

"What should I do?"

"Make your peace with God. Now, out of my way!"

Stunned, Sarah watched as he climbed the ladder to the main deck just as a terrible sound rent the air, part-scream, part-crack. It made her blood run cold. Gripping the rope, she followed him.

As she reached the deck the sound of the wind, a howling gale, roared in her ears. Standing was impossible. Only slight of frame, she was no match for the strength of the storm. Grabbing hold of a nearby post, she sank to her knees.

She could barely see anything other than the driving rain until unexpectedly the force of the wind whipped the rain from her eyes momentarily and the sight that greeted her was like nothing she had seen before. The ship was being torn asunder. Men were screaming, wounded and dying, sea water washing aboard in monstrous waves, then soaking away, carrying them with it.

Drenched, Sarah clung to the post. If it were God's will, she might yet make it to the Thirteen Colonies and her brother to start a new life.

If not, then she would be glad to see her beloved mother again in the ➝

next one. Closing her eyes and praying fervently, Sarah let go of the post.

The freezing sea water brought Sarah to her senses. She had no way to gauge how long she had been in the water but somehow the current had driven her ashore, leaving her in a deep rock pool.

Around her the storm still raged and she could hear the cries of the sailors and the terrible sound of the ship's hull breaking apart.

Refusing to look, Sarah lifted herself out of the rock pool and onto the sand. Suddenly, black shapes lit by swinging lanterns, surged onto the beach. Wreckers!

Sarah held herself still. For now, the men were running into the surf, hauling ashore the booty that was washing up from the stricken vessel. It would buy her time, but not much.

Ahead she could make out a mass of rocks, tumbled at the foot of the cliff. If she could somehow conceal herself within their depths, she thought she might yet make it through this night to see another sunrise.

The man was by her side before she had time to react, his hand over her mouth, his arm wrapped around her. He half-lifted, half-carried her towards the cliff. Sarah struggled against him, but she was no match for his strength.

"A pretty maid like you has no business on this beach tonight," he said. "Go as far as you can into the cave. Hide yourself away, my lovely. When tis safe, I will come for 'ee. Mind you stay out of sight now." He lifted his finger in warning. "Else we'll both be dead by morning."

The flickering flame of a candle and the grotesque shadow it threw up the walls of the cave alerted Sarah.

"Maid? Tis time. Show yerself."

Shaking, Sarah stepped from her hiding place. From the light of the candle, she could see for the first time the face of a young man with a thick, dark beard. Above the beard were sensitive, dark eyes. He did not have the eyes of a man who could do harm, Sarah decided.

"Where are we going?"

"My cottage. We need to be quick and we need to be quiet."

Picking up on the undercurrent of his tension, Sarah nodded.

The blackness of the night was pierced only by the lantern he held shielded against his chest. Sarah looked towards the sound of the sea.

"There's none left alive, 'cept you."

Holding her hand, the man tugged her up a sandy path, then onto steps hewn from rock. As they ran up the hillside, rock turned to coarse grass.

Topping the hill, the man turned and gave her a fleeting smile. "Not far now."

The descent was steeper than the climb. Sarah gripped the man's hand as hard as she could, afraid she would fall.

As her eyes grew accustomed to the dark, she could make out a cluster of cottages hugging the hillside down to the valley floor where the harbour lay. The stench of fish filled the air.

The man pointed towards the nearest cottage and the open back window.

Unceremoniously, he thrust her inside and Sarah found herself deposited upon a wooden settle. There was a fire roaring in the grate and two tankards set up on the table. The man appeared a few moments later through the door.

"I'm Joseph Tregonan."

"Sarah Tanner."

"Nice to make your acquaintance,

Sarah. There's a potato pie for you to eat and a drop of ale to drink." He set the food and drink before her.

"What happened on the beach?" she asked, between mouthfuls.

"A little free trade was had."

It was a euphemism Sarah recognised. "You're a smuggler."

"Aye and proud of it. The sea may be bountiful, but she can be cruel as well. The life of a Cornish fisherman is a hard one. If a bolt of lace or a keg or two of brandy can ease our ills, what harm is there? The Squire and the Parson and all those hereabouts are as much a part of the

Joseph shook his head. "My brother, though I love him dear, is a brutal man. I am not cut from the same cloth. I'll see no harm done to 'ee. Tell me, what were you doing on the ship anyhow?"

"I was sailing to the New World to be with my brother."

"A new life?" Joseph stared into the fire. "Sounds grand. We'd best get you free and clear and over the Tamar then, but until then, you and I are bound by this secret and our lives the price paid if we be discovered. Sleep awhile, you may have my bed, I've no need of it this night. Tomorrow we make good our escape."

"A new life? Sounds grand. We'd best make good our escape then, my lovely"

night-time trade as my brother an' me."

"And the sailors and passengers?"

"Perished."

"Perished how?" she was afraid to ask but she had to know.

"The sea took most of 'em."

"Most but not all?"

Joseph sighed. "My brother Jeremiah doesn't like witnesses. Dead men tell no tales, Miss. He's a rash man and he'll get himself killed one of these days, but it won't be today."

Sarah's eyes widened. "Thank you for helping me but I'll be on my way now." Rising, Sarah walked towards the door.

Joseph laughed. "And how long do you think you'll last out there, my lovely? Half the village are searching for 'ee, the other half would turn you in. Jeremiah saw you dragging yourself from the rock pool and when he turned to look again, you were gone. Spirited away by me but he did not know that."

Sarah stopped short of the door. "But you're his brother. Surely, I am in more danger within than without?"

The sunlight, piercing and strong, woke Sarah from a troubled sleep. Sometime in the night Joseph had left her a hunk of bread and tankard of water. She broke her fast listening to the raucous shouts of the villagers and the harsh cry of the gulls. She had just finished eating when she heard the cottage door open and held herself still.

"We got the cargo safely stored after you left. What ailed 'ee brother?"

"My guts weren't good."

"Truth be told, you still look pale. You'll be with us tonight, I hope? I'd have you by my side when we move the goods inland, young Joe."

"I'll be there."

"The Master says we'll see a goodly return on our night's work."

"And the Customs Men?"

"They'll be here dreckly, no doubt. Donnee worry, brother. T'ain't no one to say it was anything more than a tragic accident. All those poor souls, lost at sea. Them that knows different, knows to keep quiet, else they'll feel the blade of ➤

Jeremiah's knife across their gullet."

"And the girl?"

"Can't have gone far. I've men out looking. Why don't you join us? The fresh air will do you good, brother."

It seemed like an age until she heard footsteps on the stairs. There was nowhere to hide and if it were Jeremiah, Sarah knew she was done for.

Relief flooded through her as Joseph entered the room – carrying a dress and a shawl.

"You slept?" he asked.

She nodded.

"My mother's," he said, as he passed the clothes to her.

"Won't your mother miss them?" she asked.

"She's been

dead this past year. The coughing sickness took her."

"I'm sorry,' Sarah said.

"Tonight, we're moving the goods to the Church on the moors. Once that's done, I will be back for you. Don't look so afraid. Tis a score of wrecks I's seen these past few years and I'm still here to tell the tale. I'll see you safely to the Tamar yet. We'll journey by sea. I hope you have a strong stomach."

She nodded.

"Good, yer can hold the bucket for me, then, my lovely."

"I thought you were a fisherman? Surely, you don't get seasick?"

"Now, Mistress Tanner, I do believe I fooled 'ee," he said, with a warm chuckle.

Sarah laughed.

"Tis a pleasant sound to hear a pretty maid laugh."

She coloured.

"We'll sail to Tregelian. From there I'll find you a horse and cart Tamar-bound and you can start your new life over. Soon you'll forget about young Joe, the wrecker who spared your life."

Joseph laughed. "Now, there's a welcome to gladden the heart."

"I thought you were lost."

"The Master was late," Joseph explained. "Come, sit with me. We had a fine feast."

From his cloak he pulled a leg of roast chicken. "I saved this for you."

"When I spared you, I saved myself from damnation. Tis a fair exchange, I reckon"

"I shan't forget you," she said, quickly. "You risked your life to save mine. That's not a debt easily repaid."

He smiled. "No debt, my lovely. I've never hurt a woman, much less killed one. A price like that would weigh heavy on a man's soul. When I spared you, I spared myself from damnation. Tis a fair exchange, I reckon."

That evening as Joseph prepared to leave, he took Sarah's hands in his and sat her down.

"See here, Mistress Tanner, there's a door at the back of the cupboard which leads onto the cliff. Should I not return by the time this night is done, be gone up the cliff. Follow the path to Tregelian. It'll take you a day. Tis harsh going but donnee stop and donnee turn back. You understand?"

Sarah nodded.

Then, on impulse she kissed his cheek.

"Good luck," she told him.

For what seemed like hours, Sarah watched the single candle burn down. *Please come back to me, Joe!*

Finally, voices carried to her, indistinct, then stronger. Sarah waited upstairs until she was sure Joe was alone then she hurried down. Overcome with emotion, she flung herself into his arms.

Sarah took it gratefully and ate.

"With full bellies and full pockets, the village will sleep late today. We'll sail before dawn. Tis market day in Tregelian so we'll be sure to find you a ride."

Sarah's heart heaved.

Was it the thought of escape and the peril that went with it or was it the thought of leaving Joe behind?

The boat was smaller than she had imagined.

"Hide yourself behind the lobster pots until we are clear of the harbour. Tis a pretty moon. Make a wish, my lovely."

Shutting her eyes, Sarah made her wish as the boat cleared the harbour and turned around the headland. When she opened her eyes, she could see that Joe was watching her with a smile.

"Your turn," she said.

"Tain't no point. My wish can never come true."

"How do you know?"

"Some things aren't meant to be."

Lulled by the gentle movement of the sea, so different to the night before, Sarah dozed. The sound of the boat being hauled over cobbles, woke her.

"Is this Tregelian?"

"T'other side of the hill. We'll rest here till morning."

Fashioning his jacket into a pillow, ➤

Joseph laid down on the beach.

Taking her lead from him, Sarah settled down beside him.

"Your shawl makes a poor pillow, Mistress Tanner. My chest might serve you better."

"And your arm a blanket?" she asked, with a smile.

but once those handsome men of the Thirteen Colonies catch yer eye, you'll not care for the likes of young Joe."

"That's not true." Sarah took his hand in hers. "Come with me. You said yourself, your brother will get himself killed one day. Must you suffer the same fate? Would your poor, dead mother want

"There shall be none to gainsay us, none shall know of the secret that we share"

"If you would like?"

"I would like," she replied and settled herself against him.

For the first time since making landfall the previous night, Sarah slept soundly, safe in Joe's arms.

As the sun rose, they set off for Tregelian.

"Once you get across the Tamar, you'll be in Plymouth. Head to the harbour. There'll be plenty of boats there to take you wherever you want to go. And this will see you right." He pressed a leather pouch into her palm.

"What's this?"

"Tis my share from the night's work."

"But I can't take this." She thrust it back at him.

"I want you to have it. It came from a bad thing but something good can come of it now."

"No, you don't understand, Joe," she said. "I don't want to leave. Not anymore. Not unless you come with me. It's what I wished for on the moon, you see – that we might be together."

Joseph stroked her cheek. "You say that now, my lovely

both her sons mouldering in early graves? Or does the thought of being with me displease you so much?"

He laughed. "Does it displease me? Sarah, my darling, you could never displease me. You've held my heart fast in your hand from the first moment we met. But you deserve a good man – a better man than the likes of me."

"Bad deeds have been done, I shan't deny it," she said. "But what you did for me was not the act of a bad man but a good one."

Joseph stared at her for the longest time. "A life away from these shores? Where none shall know us?"

Sarah nodded. "You'll be a fisherman and I a seamstress and we shall be Mr and Mrs Tregonan, for there shall be none to gainsay us."

"Better that we're Mr and Mrs Tanner, I reckon, for the name Tregonan is feared in these parts and sailors might carry terrible tales of my brother to even the farthest of shores."

"Tanner it is then, and none shall know of the secret that we share, that you were once a wrecker and I the maid who stole your heart."

Brain Boosters

Missing Link

The answer to each clue is a word which has a link with each of the three words listed. This word may come at the end (eg HEAD linked with BEACH, BIG, HAMMER), at the beginning (eg BLACK linked with BEAUTY, BOARD and JACK) or a mixture of the two (eg STONE linked with HAIL, LIME and WALL).

ACROSS

7 Code, Machine, Variations (6)
8 Photography, Television, View (6)
9 Eleven, Fours, Point (4)
10 Chinese, Orange, Whitehall (8)
11 Overactive, Public, Vivid (11)
14 Artistic, Musical, School (11)
18 Conference, Power, Responsibility (8)
19 Skin, Sleep, South (4)
20 Body, Life, Welsh (6)
21 Inspector, Meal, Return (6)

DOWN

1 Passion, Rebellion, Tissues (7)
2 Ago, Dark, Middle (4)
3 Back, Joint, Steak (6)
4 Oil, Tree, Whip (6)
5 Prison, Role, Rows (5,3)
6 Fire, Recovery, Transit (5)
12 Euclidean, Plane, Set (8)
13 Market, Songs, Up (7)
15 Be, High, Worthy (6)
16 Broad, Dust, Fitted (6)
17 Conference, Reception, Sports (5)
19 Bombay, Ruddy, Weed (4)

Turn To P171-173 For Solutions

Hidden word in the shaded squares: _____

Moving On

It seemed that his ex-girlfriend Cerys was haunting her, telling her to get out of his flat… but why?

By Gillian Harvey

This time, she moved quickly, flinging the door open and stepping into the kitchen. Only her shaking hand gave away how she felt inside. Then she saw that she'd been right. A bag of flour had tipped on its side, some of the content spilling on the floor. She gasped as she read the letters, traced in the white dust by an invisible hand.

Lucy had never believed in love at first sight, but when Pete had walked into her life three months ago, she'd felt an instant jolt of connection. They'd met at a local auction house – he'd been selling, she'd been buying – and had struck up a conversation over a cup of coffee afterwards.

Suddenly she'd understood all those times her friends had disappeared in the early stages of a relationship – that

almost insatiable desire to be with the object of your affections, at the expense of everything else. Who wanted to hit the gym with their friend when they had a gorgeous man waiting to take them to dinner? Why would she pass up the chance to snuggle on the sofa with her new boyfriend to attend after work drinks?

She'd fallen hard and fast, begun dreaming of white dresses and bridal

bouquets much earlier in the relationship than was sensible, but she couldn't seem to help herself.

"He's just so perfect," she gushed to her sister on the phone. "I feel… almost as if it's meant to be!"

"Well, I'm pleased for you," Kelly said. "So, when do I get to meet him?"

It was hard living so far from family. Lucy had moved to London six months beforehand for an opportunity and barely got back to Bournemouth these days to see Kelly and the twins, let alone Mum and Dad. She missed them terribly.

"Soon, I hope," she replied, wondering if Pete might be able to take a couple of days off for a seaside break. It was difficult, with his work. He'd travel around, picking up bargains and shipping them to various auction houses.

"Your life is basically *Bargain Hunt* without the tragic sweatshirts," she'd told him once, and he'd laughed.

"He's just so perfect," she gushed to her sister. "I feel that it's meant to be!"

They seemed to share so many things – a similar sense of humour, even their dislike of milky tea – saw eye-to-eye on almost everything. Sometimes, in the early weeks, Lucy would lie in bed after they'd said goodnight, realising her mouth was aching from smiling so much.

About a month in, he sat her down and told her something that made her gasp. "I'm actually widowed," he ➡

said. "Well, I mean, I wasn't officially married. Cerys and I, we lived together though. And… well, it all happened so unexpectedly."

"Oh my god," she said, reaching for his hand instinctively.

"I didn't tell you before," he said. "Because… I dunno. I didn't want to scare you off, I guess."

"Don't be silly," she said, wrapping her arms around him. "It must have been terrible for you." Somehow his tragic past made her want to look after him, brought out her protective instincts.

She realised, too, that this was probably why after a month of dating she'd yet to see his apartment. Something that had been a niggling worry at the back of her mind. They always came back to her place. He'd make excuses and she hadn't felt able to press him. She'd wondered whether he lived with his parents, or had a messy flatmate, or was ashamed of the state of his place.

However, once she'd learned about Cerys, an invitation soon followed.

"Why not come over to mine later?" he said casually on the phone. "I'll cook."

She felt as if this invitation was somehow an admission that their relationship was more than a short-term thing, and fizzed with excitement when she knocked on the door of his second-floor flat in Brixton.

Inside, she felt a little odd when sitting on his sofa, sipping wine. Photos of Cerys still displayed on the mantlepiece made her feel as if she was stealing another woman's man, but Cerys had died over a year ago, Lucy reminded herself. It was natural that Pete would want to keep her picture around. She'd have to accept his

past as part of the overall package. So she smiled and sipped her wine and tried not to wonder whether or not Cerys had been more attractive than she was.

"She was very pretty," she ventured, when they returned to the sofa after their meal.

"Yeah," he said, wistfully looking at the picture. Then seeming to acknowledge the photos for the first time had flushed slightly. "Oh, it must be weird for you," he said. "Do you want me to turn them round or something?"

"Oh no, don't be silly," she lied. "Cerys is part of who you are – it's important to remember her."

"You're amazing," he said, leaning in for a kiss. "Although," he added, getting up, "I might turn her around for a bit. Feels somehow rude to be… you know, in front of her." He turned the frame and smiled ruefully. "It's as much for her as for us," he added. "Cerys was fantastic, but she was definitely the jealous type."

"Oh?"

"Yeah." He shrugged. "You know how it gets sometimes. Used to drive me nuts."

She decided not to press him. Instead she reached up her arms to receive his embrace and sunk again into his kiss.

They both jumped apart when the photo fell.

It was like she was trying to get rid of me," she joked later to Kelly. "Jealous ex-girlfriend haunting the new one."

"That," said Kelly, "sounds farfetched even for you."

"I'm joking really," Lucy said. "You know I don't believe in all that stuff."

Still, it was hard not to acknowledge the slightly stifled atmosphere at the flat.

The feeling of unease she experienced whenever Pete left the room. She'd shake it off, tell herself she was being paranoid, but sometimes when she'd look at the photos, she was sure she saw a hardness in Cerys' expression that hadn't been there before.

It didn't stop her jumping into Pete's arms a couple of months later when he suggested they move in together, though.

At first, when he'd asked if they could talk she'd thought he was going to break up with her. Things had changed a little over the last month, he'd been colder.

"Oh Pete!" she said. "Are you sure?" Then, "What shall we do? Sublet this and move to mine?"

"Do you mind if we stay here?" he said. "It's just that it's so convenient for the trains, and I've got that space for my van."

She'd been unable to refuse, and by the weekend they'd moved half her wardrobe and all of her essentials into his. The whether he'd shut the door properly. Groaning, she got herself out of bed to take a quick peep, saw that the door was properly closed, then staggered gratefully back to her duvet nest.

Only, when she tried to get back in, she found she couldn't lift the duvet. When she'd tried to explain it later to Kelly, she'd been unable to properly describe the strange feeling of pulling at its corner and finding it stuck to the bed as if glued. As if held in place by an invisible hand.

Then it released and she shook her head and climbed gratefully in. Seconds later, the whole incident was written off by her rational brain. It had got caught on something, or she hadn't pulled it properly. Perhaps she'd grabbed the fitted sheet by mistake and felt the resistance because of its elasticated corners, tucked firmly under the mattress.

It was hard not to notice little things after that. The time when her favourite

"She's trying to get rid of me – jealous ex-girlfriend haunting the new one"

commute to her job as a legal PA was just as simple from his, and only took 10 minutes more. Plus, she was allowed to work from home a couple of times a week.

Although it felt a little odd knowing that she was moving into a home he'd once shared with Cerys, she told herself that all houses have their history – we are all surrounded by ghosts.

Not that she believed in ghosts.

It was the third week when it happened. Pete had gone off early to beat the traffic, but Lucy had decided to get a little more sleep.

The minute he'd slammed the front door, the temperature in the bedroom seemed to drop and she wondered mug turned up in the bin and Peter had denied having put it there. Or when her toothbrush disappeared, turning up in the dusty reservoir behind the sink. The coffee that spilled over when she reached for it, or the way that she sometimes turned suddenly and saw a shadow.

It was always when Pete was out, and she wondered for a while whether she was simply uncomfortable in a new place. It took two more weeks for her even to open up properly to Kelly.

"I think," she said carefully, "that Cerys might be haunting me."

Kelly snorted. "You're not serious!"

Her tone made Lucy feel silly. "I know. I know what it sounds like," she admitted. "But it's just…" and she relayed all the ➡

little incidents to her sister. But hearing them spoken aloud made her question herself too. Spilling coffee, or dropping a toothbrush were hardly reasons to call in an exorcist!

"I think," her sister said gently. "That it sounds like you need a break. Come and see us. I'm sure Pete must be able to take time off. Or there's a great auction house in Bournemouth – he could call it a work trip if he wants."

"Good idea," Lucy replied, although she suspected already that Pete would make an excuse. So far he'd seemed reluctant to meet her family – and had only seen her friends briefly in a pub before having to rush off for some furniture related emergency. She didn't know whether he was shy, or maybe nervous to take what is often seen as an important step. She didn't feel able to push him, didn't want to set off one of his bad moods – something that had become more and more frequent.

In any case, by the end of the phone

replied, not feeling able to tell him about her horror at seeing something that couldn't possibly have happened on its own. Or at least she didn't think so. Of looking up and seeing Cerys' face smiling at her from the photo, and feeling an urgent need to get out of the flat.

"Look," she said later. "I've been thinking. Maybe we should look at renting somewhere new… together. You know, a brand-new start."

"What's brought this on?" His brow furrowed. "I thought you liked the flat."

"I do. I do. It's just…" she paused. "Don't get me wrong, but I sometimes feel…" she took a deep breath. "I sometimes feel as if I'm intruding on Cerys' territory, somehow. Like… Like I'm not welcome."

He looked at her, his face clouding over slightly in a way she'd never seen before. "Seriously?" he said.

"Well, it's how I feel."

"I think you better see a therapist or something," he said dismissively.

His ex-girlfriend had disappeared two years ago... no body had been found

call she felt reassured to the point of feeling a little foolish. Kelly was right – she'd been a bit stressed at work, and tired from moving home. She was just overthinking things.

Only, when she walked through to the living room seconds later, the laptop she'd set up for a work at home day was laying on the floor.

Good day?" Pete said when he came home at seven that evening.

"Yeah," she said. "I mean, I worked in a coffee shop in the end, so…"

"Oh?"

"Yeah, just… fancied a change," she

"Because that sounds completely insane."

"Look, don't worry," she said. "I'm probably just being stupid."

The last thing she wanted to do was fight with him. She seemed to have been doing more and more things wrong recently, upsetting him without ever meaning to.

"Yeah, you and the rest of the female population."

"Excuse me?"

"Well, you know. Women and their hysterics," he said. It was hard to tell whether he was joking.

She was so shocked at this comment that she didn't challenge him on it. But later, when she lay next to his sleeping form in bed she thought about it again. It had been an odd comment from someone as loving as Pete.

Almost a red flag.

But, she thought as she turned over, they were both tired. Who hadn't said something they didn't mean once in a while? And she'd mentioned Cerys. She knew he was still hurting.

The next day, working from home and determined to overcome her silly fears, Lucy googled Cerys' name for the first time. Cerys Knight. The search yielded little – a couple of potential Facebook pages, a clipping from a local newspaper about a curry night. She clicked back onto her word processing screen and carried on typing.

Only, in the middle of typing a legal document, her screen flicked back to the browser. She tutted and went to close it down, except there, just where the arrow of her mouse hovered, was Cerys' name. She clicked and an article came up: *Local woman missing, presumed dead.*

A shiver ran through her and she felt as if she should stop reading, but somehow she couldn't. Cerys – and a picture confirmed it was the right Cerys – had disappeared after a night out two years ago. Her boyfriend Pete had been questioned extensively by the police, but eventually released without charge.

No body had been found.

Lucy felt her throat constrict slightly at reading the news. No wonder Pete had never talked about it!

She steadied herself and tried to switch back to the document, feeling guilty for having looked. Only the document, when she switched it back, had changed.

Her four paragraphs of careful typing had been deleted and instead, the words GET OUT had been written in capital letters.

Yeah?" he said when he picked up the phone.

"Pete!" she cried and told him the story.

He was silent for a minute. Then. "Look, we need to talk about this, OK? I'll come home."

"But…?"

"I don't know what you've read, but it's all lies."

"I… I didn't think…"

"Look, I never said it before, but Cerys was a right drama queen. We hadn't been getting on well towards the end. She was losing it, I reckon. Kept saying things about me to people. About… well, accusing me of stuff."

"Oh."

"I don't know what's happening Lucy, but I reckon maybe you've picked up on some of the stress of it…"

"No, I don't…"

"Can't have you losing it too."

Then the phone went dead.

Feeling sick, she shut her laptop. Should she wait for him? Go to a café and call him back? Was she safe in the flat? Would anyone actually believe her?

A noise from the kitchen – a crash and a thump made her scream. She wanted to run – get out, just as the letters had said – but her keys were in there. Her handbag. She'd have to face whatever was there in order to escape it.

So she pushed open the door. Saw the flour, the scattering of dust on the terracotta tiles – and the words appearing as if written by a ghostly hand.

IT WAS HIM! YOU'RE NOT SAFE! GET OUT! ⓜⓦ

Rocky Road Brownies

Ingredients (Makes 24 squares)

- ◆ **200g plain chocolate, broken into pieces**
- ◆ **225g butter, cut into chunks**
- ◆ **4 eggs**
- ◆ **175g light brown muscovado sugar**
- ◆ **175g plain flour**
- ◆ **1tsp vanilla essence**
- ◆ **100g walnut halves, chopped**
- ◆ **75g white chocolate, chopped**
- ◆ **75g mini marshmallows**
- ◆ **75g chocolate drops**

1 Preheat the oven to 180°C, Fan160°C, Gas 4. Grease and line a 17x27cm tray bake tin. Place the plain chocolate and butter in a saucepan and heat gently, until melted, stirring to reduce the risk of overheating.

2 Whisk the eggs and sugar together using an electric mixer until thick and fluffy. Stir in the chocolate mix then fold in the flour, vanilla, walnuts and white chocolate.

3 Pour into the prepared tin and bake for 30-35min. When tested with a skewer the mix should not be just cooked in the centre. Quickly sprinkle over the mini marshmallows and chocolate drops. Return to the oven for 3-4min until the marshmallows start to puff up and the chocolate is shiny.

4 Leave on a wire rack to cool. When cold remove from the tin and place in an airtight container for 24 hours before cutting into squares.

RECIPES AND FOOD STYLING: JENNIE SHAPTER PHOTOGRAPHY: JON WHITAKER

Grandpa's War

How could a child hope to unlock the dark memories that Jim had kept in his heart for so many years?

By Jean Robinson

Elsie stops rolling pastry for their steak pie supper when she hears the words, "What did you do in the war, Grandpa?"

How will Jim react to Ruth's question? A question to which Elsie had never received an answer; one she had ceased to ask several months after he'd come home from the Front and she'd realised the distress it caused him.

Elsie is always at her happiest in this old Victorian kitchen, in the house she has always lived in, inherited from her parents who inherited it from theirs. She loves the old stone sink and stone floor. And the big scrubbed wooden table where she can roll up her sleeves and indulge in her favourite pastime – baking.

She loves it most when her little

him from staring at the fire crackling in the grate of the black-leaded range.

There is silence. Elsie bites back the urge to intervene. She doesn't want the child distressed. She doesn't want her husband to be put in this difficult situation.

A clear little voice comes again through the door joining the dining room with the back kitchen.

"It's Remembrance Sunday next weekend. We're learning about the war at school. We have to find out as much as we can and do a project on it. I told my teacher that my grandpa had been in it."

"So how much have you found out, then?" he asks her.

"I don't know anything. Mum said you'd know, and to ask you today."

"Ah, I see."

How will Jim cope with this request? He can hardly refuse the child. Why on earth

There is silence. Elsie doesn't want her husband to be put in this difficult situation

granddaughter, Ruth, comes for a day. Listening to her excited chatter in the next room. A lively seven-year-old with an inquisitive mind. Her visits do Jim a world of good. Bring him out of himself as he sits in his big wooden armchair beside the old oak dining table smoking his pipe. Something to take his attention and stop

did Hope tell her to ask him? But then, her daughter had probably never been aware of the problem. It wasn't something they'd ever talked about.

Since retiring, Jim spends much of his day sitting in that corner reading. He looks after his hens and is proud of the eggs they lay. He potters in his greenhouse ➡

tending the tomatoes. Then there are the solitary walks he takes each day. He's never asked Elsie to go with him. She's never suggested it; he needs this time alone.

A low voice, as if coming from the past, filters through to her ears.

"Well, now, where to start?"

Silence again. Elsie stiffens. She must stop this conversation.

"The Great War. It was a dreadful time." His voice is steady, if distant. "Brave young men fighting for their country on the battlefields of France. Millions severely wounded. Many lost their lives."

Every nerve in Elsie's body is taut as she scrapes the floury pastry from her hands and goes to stand by the connecting door.

She sees the look in Jim's eyes. His face is slowly receding into memory. He is back in the horrors of that war, in the trenches amongst the mud and stench. She'd read about it in the papers.

The child is perched on a little stool at his feet looking up at him, eyes wide, her little face screwed up in concentration.

station platform as a cold northerly wind whisked her headscarf into her face. His hand pressed to the glass of the carriage window, a grim smile contorting his features, as she waved bravely back. The train gathering steam, the guard's whistle, the slow chug-chug as it eased out of sight. Then the trudge home, tears streaming down her face, her heart breaking.

Living with her parents had given her some comfort. When she'd been at her lowest her mother would sit and hold her hand and try to reassure Elsie that one day the war would end and Jim would come home safe.

And he had. But he was a changed man. After he'd been discharged from the army he'd found it difficult to adjust to a world that had changed forever.

Slowly he had managed to get his joinery business up and running again. But he often seemed dispirited and silent. Money had been tight and it was difficult to make ends meet in the austere conditions that followed.

But there had been happy times too.

"There was so much fear, despair, longing. But also love and hope"

Elsie knows she has to let the scene play out. To stop it now would be impossible.

She listens. He continues. The child sits in silent awe.

"Aye, it was tough. Leaving your family, marching to the station, the train to Dover then across the English Channel to France. There was many a tear shed. None of us knew what would confront us there – or when we would get back."

Elsie remembers too. Shivering on the

Jim had always been a man of quiet dignity and so long as she had him home safe, Elsie could cope. They enjoyed every moment of their daughter as she grew. Jim hadn't been there at the birth. Had not seen his baby for two years. Elsie had called her Hope.

"Hunger, mud, cold wet mud, deep in the trenches," Jim continues. "We'd get parcels from home. Food, warm socks, gloves, mufflers. They were the good days. Sometimes chocolate and cigarettes. Raised

our spirits. We'd share whatever we had. We were comrades, looked out for each other. There was so much fear, despair, longing. But also love and hope. Huts close behind the firing line catered for soldiers coming and leaving the trenches or for some respite from the constant onslaught. Such kind ladies. It was like a little bit of heaven amongst all the carnage."

Elsie smiles fondly at this memory. She had knitted her share of socks for the Red Cross who delivered them to the men. She'd put love into every stitch as she imagined some poor soldier getting comfort for a while from having warm dry feet.

"Did you write letters?" Ruth asks.

"Oh, yes."

Elsie had written every day. It made her feel close to him. All the little things. Hope's first tooth, the day she toddled to her on her own two feet.

She still has some of the beautiful postcards Jim sent with pretty pictures all padded in silk. Just a sentence or two written hurriedly. *Missing my beautiful wife. Longing to see my baby girl.* So full of love. She'd held them to her heart, felt the love and couldn't stop looking at them all day.

She had no idea how he'd obtained such beautiful cards in such a place. They are wrapped in tissue paper now in a bedroom drawer. She will treasure them always.

"What happened to your arm?" Ruth questions. "Was that the war?"

Again Elsie tenses. He's sensitive about the injury. Always keeps his sleeves down to cover the scar so no one will ask him about it. She's surprised Ruth is aware of it. Hope must know more than she lets on.

He rolls up his sleeve to show Ruth the scar. Something he'd never normally do.

"That was a bad day. Continually under artillery fire. The constant noise of machine guns firing. Heavy prolonged rain turned the ground into mud. Exploding grenades forming great craters. Shrapnel flying everywhere. I caught a piece in my elbow. But I was the lucky one. I lost my best friend that day."

Elsie wants to stop him. Put an end to this ordeal. Yet still she feels it would be wrong to do so.

"Did they let you come home?"

"Yes, I was rescued by the Red Cross and given leave until it healed."

Elsie remembers how she felt when the letter arrived. She'd been anxiously waiting for one from Jim. Always looking out for the postman. Her joy when he stopped and came up the path.

Then the painful tightness in her chest as she saw that the address was not in Jim's handwriting. It was printed and official looking. How her hand had shaken as she'd torn open the envelope and the relief as the words danced in front of her eyes. He ➡

was safe. Wounded in action. He would be coming home on leave, to return to duty once the injury had healed.

She didn't let the last bit register. All she could think of was that her husband was still alive and he was coming home. She'd picked Hope from her cot and danced round the room. *Daddy's coming home.*

Jim has stopped. There's a smile on his face. A rare smile, as he looks into the upturned face of his granddaughter.

It is much later, after Hope has taken Ruth home, that they are able to talk.

"That was a difficult thing to do," Elsie says gently.

"Yes, but it had to be done."

"You didn't spare her feelings either."

"No, the child needs to know what it was really like. The horror of war. Not the glory. I had to get it across to her. There's been too much war. One after another. It has to stop. And it's our young ones we

She didn't let the last bit register. Jim was alive and he was coming home

"Plenty there to tell your teacher."

Ruth turns towards her.

"I didn't know it was like that, Grandma," the child says in a small voice. "I'm glad Grandpa came home safe."

Jim looks towards Elsie with love shining in his eyes. "I had to," he says. "Your grandmother was waiting for me."

Elsie feels her knees go weak. She manages to return to the kitchen. She rolls the pastry and places it over the dish of meat and pops it in the hot oven.

Ruth comes out to join her and is given the trimmings of the pastry to play with.

"I'm going to tell my teacher all about it on Monday," she tells Elsie with enthusiasm, not at all disturbed by what she's heard.

Elsie wonders how much the child understood. But it seems it is enough.

There is the odd glance across the dinner table but all talk of war is forgotten now as Ruth chatters on about her forthcoming birthday and who she is inviting to her party.

have to look to. It's up to me now to make sure Ruth never goes through what we did. I'm pleased she's showing an interest."

Three weeks later as they eat dinner Jim falls silent. Elsie tenses. He'd been so much happier since his talk with Ruth.

"What is it, dear?" she asks.

He looks up to face her. Taking a deep breath he gets the words out. "I think I'd like to visit some of the war graves."

"Won't it upset you again?" Elsie asks in alarm, ever concerned for his feelings.

"Yes – but it's time to say goodbye to old comrades."

"You might not find the names you're looking for," she says cautiously.

"We were all in it together, my love. Some won't even have graves. We buried them where we could. I'd like to be there were some are laid to rest. Bow my head for a moment and remember the others."

Elsie nods her understanding. She will be with him all the way. He is finally confronting his demons. The future will be different now for both of them.

Brain Boosters

Sudoku

	2			6		1		
			2			7		
		1	9		4	6		
1		3			2			
		8	7	4				
		8			5			6
	2	9		1	8			
	3			4				
	8		5			9		

Fill in each of the blank squares with the numbers 1 to 9, so that each row, each column and each 3x3 cell contains all the numbers from 1 to 9.

Word Wheel

Turn To P171-173 For Solutions

You have ten minutes to find as many words as possible using the letters in the wheel. Each word must be three letters or more and contain the central letter. Use each letter once and no plurals, foreign words or proper nouns are allowed. There is at least one nine-letter word.

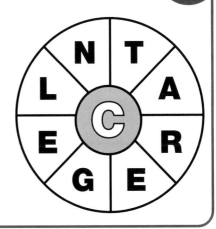

Average: 30 words
Good: 40-59 words
Excellent: 60-78 words

One Person's Junk

Far from being rubbish, the boxful of old tin badges started a chain reaction no one could even have guessed...

By Julie Dawn Baker

"How's the downsizing going?" Kate asked Marion as the two old friends sat drinking coffee in their favourite café.

Marion rolled her eyes and put down her mug. "A bit of a nightmare."

"Oh no, problems with your buyer?"

"Nothing like that. The sale and purchase seem to be moving ahead." Marion held up crossed fingers.

She and her husband, Gary, had been trying to sell their family home for a while, having found a retirement flat that would be perfect for them.

"It's all a bit stressful moving from a big house into a smaller place."

"You having second thoughts?"

Marion shook her head. "No. We don't need all that space, and it costs a fortune

enclosed the word in crooked finger air quotes. "Stuff that I find I don't want to part with."

"Isn't there storage at the new apartment?" Kate said.

"Not big enough to hold all the boxes lurking in our loft!"

Kate laughed. "I can only imagine! I haven't been in ours for years, but I know it's crammed to the rafters, literally. It's one of the reasons we keep hanging on in the house even though the girls have left. I can't face the upheaval of having to sort everything out. And Ian is worse than me for hoarding 'stuff.'" Kate repeated Marion's gesture. The word in air quotes covered a plethora of possibilities.

"What I need is a professional organiser," Marion said. "Someone who's not attached to my junk. Oh!" Her fingers

"Everything I've kept has a memory attached to it – it's treasure, not junk!"

to heat, not to mention trying to keep up with the garden. You know we're not keen gardeners. Moving will free up some of the equity in the house, so we can do the travelling we've always dreamed about. It's definitely time to move on ..." She trailed off and gazed out the window.

"But?" Kate prompted.

"But... there's so much 'stuff'," Marion

flew to her lips. "I can't believe I said that! Don't tell Gary I called it junk! He keeps saying, 'We've got to tackle the junk.' But it's not junk – it's treasure. Everything I've kept over the years has a memory attached to it. Gary says I'm being too sentimental. If he had his way, he'd take it all to the tip! And Jon's just as bad!"

When Marion had asked her adult son

if he wanted any of the keepsakes from his childhood that she'd saved for him, he'd been quick to tell her, "Thanks, but no thanks."

"He didn't even want his sports trophies," Marion said. "Neither of them understands that they're asking me to get rid of the past."

"Sacrilege! We can't have that!" Kate, whose husband was curator of the local museum, was genuinely appalled. "I tell you what – I'll come and help you," Kate offered. "I've watched loads of those programmes on TV about organising … and every episode of *Antiques Roadshow.*

I'm not sure I'll be much good at decluttering or spotting treasures, but I'm happy to give you some moral support."

"That would be great. Thanks, Kate." Marian seized the offer. It would be good to have a friend in her corner.

The next day, Marion and Kate couldn't stop giggling as, armed with a supply of heavy-duty bin bags, they scaled the pulldown ladder to the loft.

"This is another reason why I avoid our loft," Kate laughed as Marion helped to haul her into the roof space, which thankfully had been boarded so that ➡

they could move around without fear of putting a foot through the ceiling below.

"Wow! This is impressive," Kate said, taking in the shelving units housing rows of neatly labelled storage containers. "You're already so well organised! I was looking forward to channelling my inner Marie Kondo, but I think the lovely Marie would be impressed with this, too. Maybe we should pop over to my place, and you can help me sort out my loft instead!"

"We did a big clear out of all the old household things stored up here before we put the house on the market. What's left are the things that have sentimental value. Like my record collection."

Marion walked over to one of the shelves and flipped open the lid of a stripy plastic case to reveal a cache of LPs. She pulled out the first one – it was *Cherish* by David Cassidy.

"This was one of the very first records I ever bought," Marion said, hugging it against her chest. "Gary wanted to sell all our vinyl, but I remember so fondly playing these albums on my parents' old record player…"

"But do you play them now?" Kate interrupted.

"Well, we haven't got a record player, but we could get one. They're making a comeback, you know," Marion said.

Kate eyed all the record storage cases.

"Oh, your Saturday games nights! The kids used to love those!" Kate smiled.

"They did. I was keeping the games to play with Ollie, but we don't see as much of him as we used to."

Since Jon's recent divorce, Marion's eight-year-old grandson, Ollie, only saw his dad every other weekend and the odd weeknight. All of them were finding it hard to come to terms with the new arrangement. "I'm not sure Ollie will be a fan of board games anyway. Last time they were over, he sat on the sofa engrossed in a video game on Jon's phone the whole time they were here."

"Things are different than when our kids were young," Kate said. "Let's leave the games for now, but I'd be tempted to keep some of these."

Kate moved the boxes to one side, and Marion picked up another plastic container that rattled as the contents shifted around.

Carefully prising open the lid, she smiled as light from the overhead bulb glinted on precious metal and the gleaming rainbow-coloured gems inside.

"What have we here?" Kate asked, peeking at Jon's badge collection.

"I'd forgotten all about these," Marion said as she sifted through the badges and produced an oversized blue one which proudly declared: *I am 7!*

"Sorry, Mum, I don't want the badges. I'm not a kid anymore," he told her

"They'd take up a lot of room, though. I'm sorry, but I'm with Gary on this one."

"I suppose you'll say these have to go too," Marion said sadly, when they found a box full of old board games. "You, Ian, and the girls will have played these with us in years gone by," she added, hoping to engender some sympathy.

As time went on, both women started dipping into the assortment, pulling out badges commemorating birthdays, visits to sporting events, local attractions, theme parks, and holidays farther afield.

Kate held up a badge from Disney World Florida.

"Lucky Jon! He's got souvenirs from all over. You took him to a lot of places!"

"We were always doing something. We'd pack a picnic and make a day of it."

"Hey!" Kate retrieved a large, rectangular orange badge with an image of the O2 and *Dome 2000* written on it. "Oh, remember you and I took the kids to the Millennium Dome together! What a great day out that was!"

"So many happy memories," Marion said wistfully.

"These badges represent years of experiences, and more than a decade of outings with Jon. A whole social history," Kate murmured, a note of appreciation in her voice and a sparkle in her eyes.

"Honestly, Kate, I can't bear to part with these."

"Why don't you check with Jon again – show him these," Kate advised. "He might surprise you."

Marion phoned her son that evening. "Sorry Mum, there's no room in my flat for junk, and I don't want the badges anyway. I'm not a kid anymore," he reminded her.

"I know," she said, trying not to sound disappointed.

She'd brought the box of badges down from the loft and had been absently looking through them as she talked to Jon.

Coming upon a souvenir from the National Motor Museum, she said, "As you've got Ollie this weekend, how about we all go for a day out…"

Again, she was disappointed. After chatting a bit longer, Marion hung up and looked at Gary with a sigh.

"Jon didn't want to go to Beaulieu on the weekend then?" Gary asked.

"No. He's taking Ollie and some of his friends to Laser Quest. Apparently, Ollie thinks it's boring being at Jon's new place, so he feels under pressure to find exciting things to do. I don't know why they always involve technology though," she muttered.

"To be fair, we used to take Jon to the laser place with his mates," Gary said.

"I know," Marion agreed, still rummaging through the badges.

Finding what she was looking for, Marion waved the shiny disc triumphantly.

"And I have the badge to prove it!"

Moments later, Marion's phone dinged signalling a text. Marion read it and smiled to herself.

"Jon changed his mind?" Gary asked.

"No, that was Kate. Ian's putting together a new display at the museum, called Childhood through the Decades. It's focusing on what it was like to be a child in the area during different time periods, and Jon's badge collection might make ➤

"They're on a mission to visit together all the places his dad went to as a boy"

a useful addition. Ian wants to see it!"

"Now, don't go getting your hopes up, Marion, it's only a bunch of old badges, after all" Gary said.

Museum curator Ian, however, did not agree with Gary's assessment, and was thrilled with the collection, which according to Ian was "an excellent representation of one boy's experience of the nineties."

Jon hadn't been quite as thrilled as Marion by this development. She'd had to persuade her son to let the museum use some old photos of him, and he'd been very reluctant to be interviewed by Ian's assistant. Luckily, however, he'd agreed in the end.

Several months later, Marion and Gary were finally installed in their new apartment when Kate stopped by for coffee. In a little dish sitting on the coffee table, she spied a badge. "Beaulieu… National Motor Museum… Is this one we missed?" Kate asked her friend.

"No, I bought it for Ollie at the weekend. We all had a lovely day out there. To be honest, Ollie wasn't bothered about getting a badge, but I bought one anyway. I thought I'd start my own little collection for him. After all, Jon ended up being quite pleased I'd kept his all these years." Marion chuckled. "Who would have thought that discovering those badges would set off such a chain of positive events?"

"How's that?"

"Well, Ollie's school

organised a trip to the museum, and he was so proud of his dad for having a starring role in Ian's new exhibition – Jon being "Mr 90s" – that he made Jon go back to the museum to take pictures of his badges. They made a list, and now they're on a mission to visit all of the places Jon went to as a boy. These days, Ollie is actually eager to stay at Jon's on the weekends."

"How lovely! Ian said he'd seen Jon and Ollie at the museum quite a bit lately… although I'm not entirely sure it's always to see the display," Kate said.

"No, I believe there's a certain curator's assistant who's proving quite the attraction."

"Laura! She's a gem! Ian might have mentioned that she and Jon seemed to be getting on rather well."

"They're going on a date this Saturday," Marion confided. "It's good to see Jon getting out, and we get Ollie for a sleepover! Lucky you let me keep some of those board games. Fingers crossed he enjoys them."

"And what about you and Gary?" Kate asked, taking a sip of her coffee. "Any plans to start travelling?"

"Well, Ollie seems quite keen on the idea of a trip to Disney World. It's on their list, you see."

"Would you go again?"

"Definitely! One of the reasons for downsizing was so we could travel. And besides, think of all the badges I could get to add to Ollie's collection!" **MW**

Brain Boosters

Kriss Kross

Try to fit all the listed words back into the grid.

Turn To P171-173 For Solutions

4 letters
HILT
MAMA

7 letters
BOROUGH
PALAZZO

8 letters
UNHARMED
WORKSHOP

9 letters
BLUEPRINT
LIBRARIAN

10 letters
ACCUMULATE
AUCTIONEER
TORRENTIAL

11 letters
BEACHCOMBER
COMRADESHIP
REORIENTATE

Santa's Secret

When you're eight and asking for a seriously ambitious present, things might not happen quite as you expect…

By Glynis Scrivens

It was three o'clock on Christmas morning. The house was freezing and dark as Joel Johnson slipped downstairs to check his stocking.

His heart sank. The stocking was empty; he could immediately see that. What had he expected? At eight years old, he knew it was physically impossible for Santa to get a bicycle down their chimney. He'd even given it a thorough check before posting his letter to Santa. So why hadn't he asked for something else? Something that might fit down a chimney?

His little sister had asked for a doll. Ava's stocking bulged. He couldn't help himself; Joel peeped inside. In the dim light he could see that Santa had left her a baby doll. He could also make out some books. There seemed to be a ball as well.

Wretchedly disappointed, he went back to bed, knowing it was his own fault that his stocking was empty. This had never happened before.

Ava was sitting contentedly on the sofa, arms wrapped around the baby doll, her hand stroking its face in wonder. Her stocking was beside her, the other presents as yet unopened.

"Santa didn't come to me," Joel said bleakly. "My Christmas stocking's empty." He was aware of his bottom lip trembling but didn't seem able to stop it.

His father looked surprised. "Are you sure? Let's have a look."

Joel sipped his hot chocolate. There was no hurry. He knew the stocking was empty. Anyone could see that. After he'd scooped up the marshmallows one at a time and eaten them, he went over to the fireplace to join his father.

"See?" He shrugged.

His father took the stocking off its peg and handed it to Joel.

"Have you looked inside?" he asked.

Why didn't his father understand?

Joel put his hand inside, to prove there was nothing there. But to his surprise, he felt a piece of paper. As he drew it out, he

Ava laughed as Joel checked the tree again. Then he looked behind the sofa

When Joel surfaced again, it was nearly eight o'clock. He put on his dressing gown. His mother made him hot chocolate, adding three marshmallows to cheer him up.

"What's wrong with you this morning?" asked his father, who was sitting by the fire in his blue tartan dressing gown, a cup of coffee in his hand.

felt the first surge of excitement.

Santa had written him a note, in green ink. There was a drawing of a boy on a bicycle. What did this mean? Dare he hope after all?

The note read:

Your presents are playing seek and find
To get them you must use your mind:
Hiding place one has letters three

It's made of product from a tree.
Joel looked at them all excitedly.

"Santa's hidden my presents!" he yelled. "You'll have to help me find them." He started reading the note out to them.

"Product from a tree?" Mum said. "That could be sap, maybe?"

Joel loved maple syrup. But that wasn't a Christmas present, was it?

Dad grinned. "Or paper?"

"No. It's only got three letters." Joel looked around. His eyes fell on a red box under the Christmas tree, pushed to the back. He hadn't seen it there last night. Had Santa left it there?

He started tearing the box open, hope surging inside him.

It was a bicycle helmet. Smiling broadly, he put it on. Surely this meant there'd be a bicycle after all? But where could Santa have hidden it?

"Are there any more clues, Joel?" Mum asked, sipping her coffee.

Joel read aloud, "*Present two is in this room. Look behind your mother's broom.*"

The broom? That was kept in the laundry. Wasn't it?

Ava laughed as Joel checked under the tree again. Eventually he thought to look behind the sofa. The broom lay between the sofa and the wall. Putting his hand down, Joel found a bag. He pulled out a pair of snowflake patterned gloves. He put them on. They felt cosy.

"So where's my bicycle?" he asked.

Dad shrugged. "Are there any more clues?"

Joel read, "*Present three hides in plain sight. Open the door and then turn right. Rhyme with me for where it leans, decked up in gold and reds and greens.*"

Joel had no idea what Santa meant. He read it again, to himself, to see if it made any more sense. It didn't.

Mum looked puzzled. "Where has Santa left your bicycle, Joel?" she asked.

He read the clue a third time, out loud this time.

"Well, it must be outside," he said. 'I have to open the door. That must mean the front door."

With his parents beside him, and Ava dawdling behind with her doll, Joel stepped outside. What rhymed with 'me'? And then he saw it.

Ava shrieked excitedly, clapping her hands. She'd seen it too. Dad held his phone up to get a photo.

Joel's bicycle was leaning against a tree in the garden, decorated with gold, red and green tinsel.

Quail Eggs & Prawn Filo

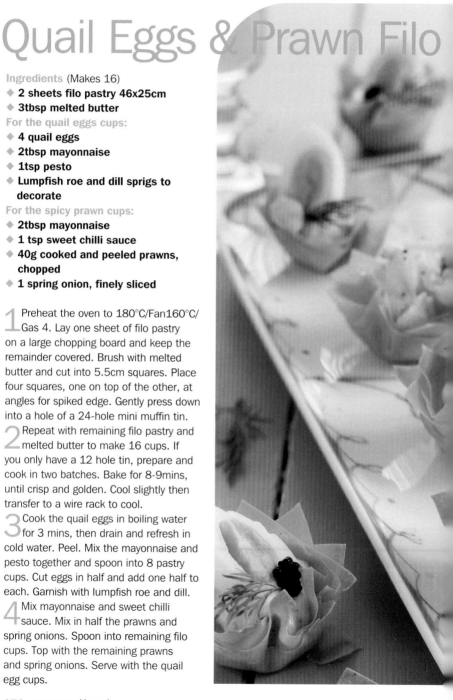

Ingredients (Makes 16)

- **2 sheets filo pastry 46x25cm**
- **3tbsp melted butter**

For the quail eggs cups:
- **4 quail eggs**
- **2tbsp mayonnaise**
- **1tsp pesto**
- **Lumpfish roe and dill sprigs to decorate**

For the spicy prawn cups:
- **2tbsp mayonnaise**
- **1 tsp sweet chilli sauce**
- **40g cooked and peeled prawns, chopped**
- **1 spring onion, finely sliced**

1 Preheat the oven to 180°C/Fan160°C/ Gas 4. Lay one sheet of filo pastry on a large chopping board and keep the remainder covered. Brush with melted butter and cut into 5.5cm squares. Place four squares, one on top of the other, at angles for spiked edge. Gently press down into a hole of a 24-hole mini muffin tin.

2 Repeat with remaining filo pastry and melted butter to make 16 cups. If you only have a 12 hole tin, prepare and cook in two batches. Bake for 8-9mins, until crisp and golden. Cool slightly then transfer to a wire rack to cool.

3 Cook the quail eggs in boiling water for 3 mins, then drain and refresh in cold water. Peel. Mix the mayonnaise and pesto together and spoon into 8 pastry cups. Cut eggs in half and add one half to each. Garnish with lumpfish roe and dill.

4 Mix mayonnaise and sweet chilli sauce. Mix in half the prawns and spring onions. Spoon into remaining filo cups. Top with the remaining prawns and spring onions. Serve with the quail egg cups.

Cups

RECIPES AND FOOD STYLING: JENNIE SHAPTER
PHOTOGRAPHY: JON WHITAKER

Keeping Traditions

Kiki didn't want to feel homesick this Christmas... but Tom always knew how to make things better

By **Kathy Schilbach**

So, Kiki, all set for next Saturday?"
"Absolutely." She laughed, the
Morris bells on her shoes jingling as she
slid along the pub bench, making room for
the others. "Dancing my first Boxing Day
stand with you guys – I'm really excited!"

She was breathless after the dress
rehearsal. There were twelve of them
– the Village Morrisettes – squashed
together round a large table in a side
room of the Red Lion.

"We'll be dancing outside so don't
forget to wear your thermals, ladies,"
Stella said, handing mugs of hot mulled
apple juice round.

Kiki sat back, smiling, happy to let the
conversation buzz all around her. Cradling
the mug of apple juice between her hands
she inhaled its spicy scent and took the
occasional sip.

From the other room came the sounds
of laughter and accordion music, the
rhythmic thump of clogs and the thud as
ten wooden staves struck the floor. The
menfolk – The Village Morris Men – were
performing the story of Saint George
slaying the dragon. When they finished
their rehearsal they'd re-join the women.
And then she'd be with Tom again. A thrill
of anticipation rushed down her spine. He
was serious but fun, strong but sensitive –
and she was falling in love with him.

A log shifted in the fireplace. She
looked across and saw the mistletoe
twined with ivy and holly along the
mantelpiece. Hmm, a kiss under the
mistletoe. Her smile held more than a
hint of mischief. How she liked these
Christmas traditions.

High in the sky, a shooting star flared.
"You know, if we were in Nigeria,"
Kiki said, breath hovering white in →

the still air, "people would be letting off firecrackers – more and more of them the closer you get to Christmas."

They'd both changed out of their Morris outfits and into warm coats, hats and scarves, and Tom was walking her back to the house she shared with three other young professionals since moving into the village six months ago.

"Another tradition." Tom drew her round to face him. "Just like the tradition of you going home to your mum and dad for Christmas."

"I'm staying in London this year. We won't be heading off to spend Christmas with my aunties and uncles in Nigeria –" She broke off, conscious of the wistful note in her voice. "You know, I'm really going to miss the firecrackers. And the Masquerades – entertainers in the villages. They wear weird clothes and dance."

"Sounds just like us."

"Even weirder. And scary. They wear masks of woven raffia or carved wood."

"I don't like to see you all sad like this." He spoke softly, and she could hear the concern in his voice.

"Hey, it's OK I'll be with Mum and Dad. And I'll be back on Boxing Day."

In the star-lit darkness she saw his gaze move slowly over her features. "I'm going to miss you."

Her heart swooped. Their relationship was new, fragile – but already she sensed this man was special to her, very special.

"I'm going to miss you too," she breathed as their lips met in a kiss as sweet and delicious as the one they'd shared beneath the Red Lion's mistletoe.

"Ah, ma chère! You were wond-air-ful!" Grinning, Tom pulled Kiki to him and gave her two extravagant air-kisses.

She laughed. "Getting into your role, I see." He had the hammiest French accent!

It was Boxing Day morning, and she and the other women had just finished their series of dances in the courtyard outside the Red Lion. The men were gathering, ready to put on their play. In his role as the dastardly Frenchman, Tom wore rouge, lipstick and a powdered wig.

"You won't go wandering off, will you?" he said.

"No, of course not," she replied just as a prolonged burst of accordion music announced the play was about to begin.

"You've got to go. Have fun, Tom".

Everyone cheered when Saint George in his white tabard with its red cross came out, and booed when his rival the Frenchman – Tom – joined him. The two men stepped back, arms outstretched. The dragon was about to make its dramatic appearance.

"Oh!" Kiki's heart did a crazy thump. Three men in a line, holding hands, danced out of the pub. Each wore a wooden mask painted in gaudy reds and golds and blues. Long thick strands of raffia and ribbon streamed from them, swirling every time the men leapt around or stooped down.

"Just like the Masquerades," she breathed.

"I went online," Tom said, joining her when the play was over. "Found plenty of photos. I had a week to make them. The others all pitched in."

"Oh Tom." Her heart was full.

"I could see how much it meant to you," he said, drawing her close.

"Yes," she said. Her throat ached with emotion. Her instincts had been right: Tom was indeed very special. **MW**

Brain Boosters

Codeword

Each letter of the alphabet has been replaced by a number. The numbers for the first name of our chosen celebrity are given. Complete the puzzle to reveal in which hit prison drama Claire King played wing governor Karen.

24	1	10	20	25	7	19	18	25	1	17		3	1	21
9		8		17		7		18		25		8		1
17	9	7	1	17		10	19	2	18	14	16	13	8	7
25		7		14		2				24		13		13
24 **C**	7 **L**	19 **A**	25 **I**	16 **R**	14 **E**		7	25	10	14	21	19	2	22
		22								2		7		1
2	25	2	19	7						18	1	13	8	
20														17
16	19	5	14							26	25	11	14	12
25		25		2								19		
18	25	17	24	18	8	16	14		2	14	23	8	25	17
6		15		16				25		11		17		19
14	4	20	16	14	2	2	14	12		19	24	18	14	12
16		25		19		1		7		12		14		25
2	8	17		10	1	17	14	9	7	14	17	12	14	16

A B C D E F G H I J K L M N O P Q R S T U V W X Y Z

1	2	3	4	5	6	7 **L**	8	9	10	11	12	13
14 **E**	15	16 **R**	17	18	19 **A**	20	21	22	23	24 **C**	25 **I**	26

Turn To P171-173 For Solutions

3	19 **A**	12		15	25 **I**	16 **R**	7 **L**	2

Where The Heart Is

I loved my contented country life, here in my home village. But could I afford to stay?

By Barbara Featherstone

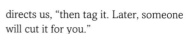

"We're almost here, Kyle!" I breathe, excitedly. "Look, it's signposted: *CHRISTMAS TREE FARM. First left.*"

Kyle turns the Jeep into a long, muddy lane and parks neatly in an equally muddy patch allotted for visitors. As we emerge into a squelchy puddle, I'm thankful that we opted for wellies and old clothes for this expedition.

It's two weeks until Christmas. The farm is busy, filled with seasonal excitement, smiling families, children's laughter, and the sharp scent of fir. Neither I nor Kyle have visited a Christmas tree farm before, so we call in for some guidance at a nearby log cabin, set up as an office.

Inside, it is warm and cosy, festooned with red-berried holly, coloured tinsel, carved figures of elves and reindeer, and miniature Christmas stockings.

A friendly assistant advises us on safety issues, the various types of tree available at the farm, and gives us a leaflet on the care of a live Christmas tree. Kyle and I always have a real tree for Christmas – a small one for Kyle's bijou flat, and a larger one for my cottage. But any extra information is always welcome.

"Choose your tree," the assistant directs us, "then tag it. Later, someone will cut it for you."

Kyle asks for two tags as we need two trees. The assistant notes down some details, then hands us the tags.

"I hope you and your wife find exactly what you're looking for," he says, cheerfully. "Happy hunting!"

"Wife…?" I mutter under my breath and go a bit pink at the guy's mistake. Kyle simply grins and tucks my arm in his.

Lacy snowflakes are drifting softly as we make our way through the thicket of trees. Some of the families we encounter I recognise from our village. And several of the children are from the village primary school where I teach.

"Happy Christmas, Miss Taylor!" they chirrup. One cheeky little girl called Evie points at Kyle.

"Is he your boyfriend, Miss Taylor?"

My blush deepens. Kyle Lawrence, local estate agent, is a tall, handsome guy with these wicked blue eyes and a half-tilted smile. He was born – like me – in our small, close-knit Dorset village. I feel as if I've known him since for ever.

Kyle and I are close friends, for the last few months teetering on the brink of

Kyle gazes at them, wistfully, then turns to me. "What more could you ask for, Gabby? Christmas trees, snow, children, laughter and fun." He winks at me and slants me this mysterious look. "I wonder what Santa will bring you."

I feel the sudden prick of tears. Kyle draws me gently to him.

Wife? I go pink at the mistake. Kyle simply grins and tucks my arm into his

something more. But Kyle likes slow and cautious. And I'm thinking suddenly that time is about to run out.

A little way into the thicket is an enchanted Santa's grotto, strung with jewelled fairy lights. A queue is already forming, small children seated on their fathers' shoulders.

"What is it, Gabby?" he asks.

I shake my head. I don't want to spoil the magic of the morning. We wander on, admiring all the beautiful trees.

After a great deal of debate, I plump for a six-foot Nordmann Fir and Kyle opts for a small Norway Spruce. We return to a little café near the office where we order hot apple cider and wait for our trees ➔

to arrive. Another friendly assistant nets them and helps Kyle load them on the roof rack of the Jeep.

Back at the cottage, Kyle carries my tree into the sitting room, erects it and helps me to decorate it. I know he is waiting for an explanation of my distress at the farm earlier, so we sit together on the sofa, Kyle's arm about me, and I tell him how it is…

Three years ago, I inherited my beloved grandmother's apricot-washed cottage and its rambling garden. The cottage is a century old, full of charm and memories. But the upkeep is hard on a young teacher's salary.

This village is where I belong, but I may have to move away; property rarely comes up for sale. It will break my heart to leave. But I have to sell. I ask Kyle to put my cottage on the market.

Kyle is silent for a while. He frowns.

"I have to get back to work now," he says. "We"ll speak this evening, Gabby."

An hour later, he's on the phone to me, brisk and professional. He has a Mr and Mrs Yates with him in the office, from London, visiting friends. They are considering swapping city life for the countryside.

scrubbed, tidied, now immaculate kitchen.

Mr Y is short and wiry, dressed in tight blue jeans and pink T. His leather jacket is hooked, casual-like, about his shoulders. He sports a long, greying pigtail and a fake tattoo sleeve. In my mind I nickname him "Pigtail Joe".

Lou-Lou Darling is a plump nutshell of a woman with a prim, thin mouth. She is squeezed into a blue woollen coat a size too small and a tad too short.

"It's small." Her voice scratches.

"Small," he says.

"And there's no island." The thin lips purse. "I want an island."

"Island…"

"The whole kitchen needs gutting and remodelling."

"Gutting…"

"We'll have granite worktops, of course."

"Granite…"

"And dark oak units. Cream is too – country, you know?"

But this is a country cottage. I feel a prickle of resentment. Their voices fade as I gaze out of the kitchen window, a few snowflakes drifting in the half-light. The village lights begin to flicker, the huddle of cottages a friendly glow.

Kyle edges close to me, his voice low.

"Your news took me by surprise this

Lou-Lou Darling looks pointedly at the scattering of needles beneath the tree

They called at Kyle's office on a whim. Would a viewing be convenient? Kyle asks. They could be with me in ten.

My first thought is "no". There's barely time to tidy. But with the worry of winter heating bills, I change my mind.

But could you live with it, Lou-Lou, darling?" Mr Yates asks his wife. He glances dubiously about my frantically

morning, Gabby. I thought it was only right to introduce you to the Yateses. But we need to talk."

"Our white goods won't fit in here. We'll need to buy new." Lou-Lou Darling's edginess breaks us apart.

"Everything you see is included in the sale, Mrs Yates," I inform her.

She has this sour look.

"We'll buy new," she repeats. "Top

of the range." She frowns. "I don't see a spin drier or dish washer anywhere."

I dry my washing on the line. And I wash up the old-fashioned way.

"Spin drier, dish washer…" Pigtail Joe ticks off on his fingers.

"Make a list," hisses Lou-Lou Darling.

"List…" He rifles in his pocket for a slim notepad and stubby pencil.

"Let me show you the sitting room, Mr and Mrs Yates," says Kyle, pleasantly.

I pad after them. There's the sharp tang of the Christmas tree and the twinkle of lights. Gran always had a live tree and I've kept up the tradition. Live trees are beautiful; they breathe.

"Villagers leave their curtains open at Christmas time," Kyle explains to the London couple. "Then everyone can enjoy the fairy lights and decorations."

Lou-Lou Darling looks pointedly at the scattering of needles beneath the tree.

"We prefer an artificial tree."

Kyle diverts her attention to the pretty leaded windows, the inglenook fireplace where yellow-red flames dance with the scent and crackle of apple wood.

"An open fire is great in winter," he smiles. "You can cosy up with a book."

"Books…" mutters Pigtail Joe.

"Reading wastes time," snarls Lou-Lou Darling, lips curling.

There's a hasty scribbling out.

"And open fires are messy – raking out the ashes, smut everywhere. We'll buy a new living flame gas fire."

"There is no gas," I slip in sweetly. "The cottage is all electric. But you could enquire about having gas laid on. It'll mean running a pipe from the lane, mind. It'll cost a bit, that will."

What am I doing? I'm supposed to be talking up the cottage, not talking it down!

"Gas pipe…" Pigtail Joe moistens the tip of his pencil.

Kyle leads the way upstairs. There are two double bedrooms; we enter mine. My nightdress lies crumpled on the bed. Absentmindedly, Kyle folds it and tucks it beneath the pillow. I feel myself blush.

"But I wanted an en suite. I told you," huffs Lou-Lou Darling.

"En suite…."

The guy will run out of space soon.

We move to the second bedroom.

"A delightful guest room, Mr and Mrs Yates, "suggests Kyle. "Or… a baby's nursery, perhaps," he adds softly, for my ears only. "In time, of course."

I glance at him, startled. A nursery…?

The blue of his eyes deepens as his gaze meets mine. ➜

My bathroom is a non-starter. Ivory is out, apparently; white is in. Yellow walls? Nah, grey is in vogue.

The separate toilet is also a no-go; a combined bathroom the latest thinking.

But when you're soaking in the bath and someone's desperate for the loo…

We traipse back downstairs.

Lou-Lou Darling frowns. "These stairs squeak. The doors squeak, too."

I smile, politely.

"It's a kind of Morse code. You can hear if burglars are coming."

Kyle stifles a snort.

"Burglar alarm," anticipates Pigtail Joe.

"And now the garden," says Kyle.

In the falling dusk, shrubs and foliage are snow-spangled and mysterious.

"I'll tell them you have a more tempting offer." He strides across to the Yates. "Erm, sorry folks…"

The bell ringers start up, practising for the Christmas services.

"In the countryside," sniffs Lou-Lou Darling, frostily, "one does expect to enjoy peace and quiet."

"Hah!" snorts Pigtail Joe. "Remember that raucous cockerel this morning, and that noisy herd of cows we passed?"

Lou-Lou Darling's eyes narrow.

"I counted five horrid cow pats in the lane." She shudders and turns to us decisively. "Thank you for the viewing. But the countryside is NOT for us!"

Kyle escorts them to their car and they roar off down the lane.

I smile politely. "It's a kind of Morse code. You can hear if burglars are coming"

"There are hollyhocks, marigolds and roses in summer," I state, dreamily.

"This garden is untidy and overgrown," declares Lou-Lou Darling.

But can't you see? It's a wildlife garden. It provides food and shelter for birds, insects, frogs, squirrels…

"We'll level it. An infinity lawn, I think."

"Infinity lawn…"

The viewing is at an end. The Yates wander off to confer, Pigtail Joe flourishing the list. Snatches of conversation filter across. "… modernisation, redecoration, refurbishing…"

"They're going to make a cheeky offer," predicts Kyle. He sounds strangely cheerful. I clutch at his arm.

"I can't sell to these people, Kyle. Whoever moves into my darling cottage must love it as much as I do."

Kyle nods.

A more tempting offer? Oh yes? Really?" I tease as he returns.

To my astonishment, Kyle draws a small crimson, velvet-covered box from his jacket pocket.

"An offer which I very much hope you'll accept," he murmurs softly.

The nestled diamond glints like fire in the snowy starlight.

"I love you, Gabby," Kyle whispers as he slips the ring onto my finger. "And I love your cottage, too. I would never let you give it up unwillingly."

I glance back at the cottage. Kyle and I will be so happy here together.

"Oh, I forgot," Kyle murmurs. "The small matter of my commission."

"Your commission…?"

His blue eyes sparkle.

"A kiss, I thought."

And amid the hush of falling snow and the joyful peal of the distant Christmas bells, his mouth meets mine. Ⓜ

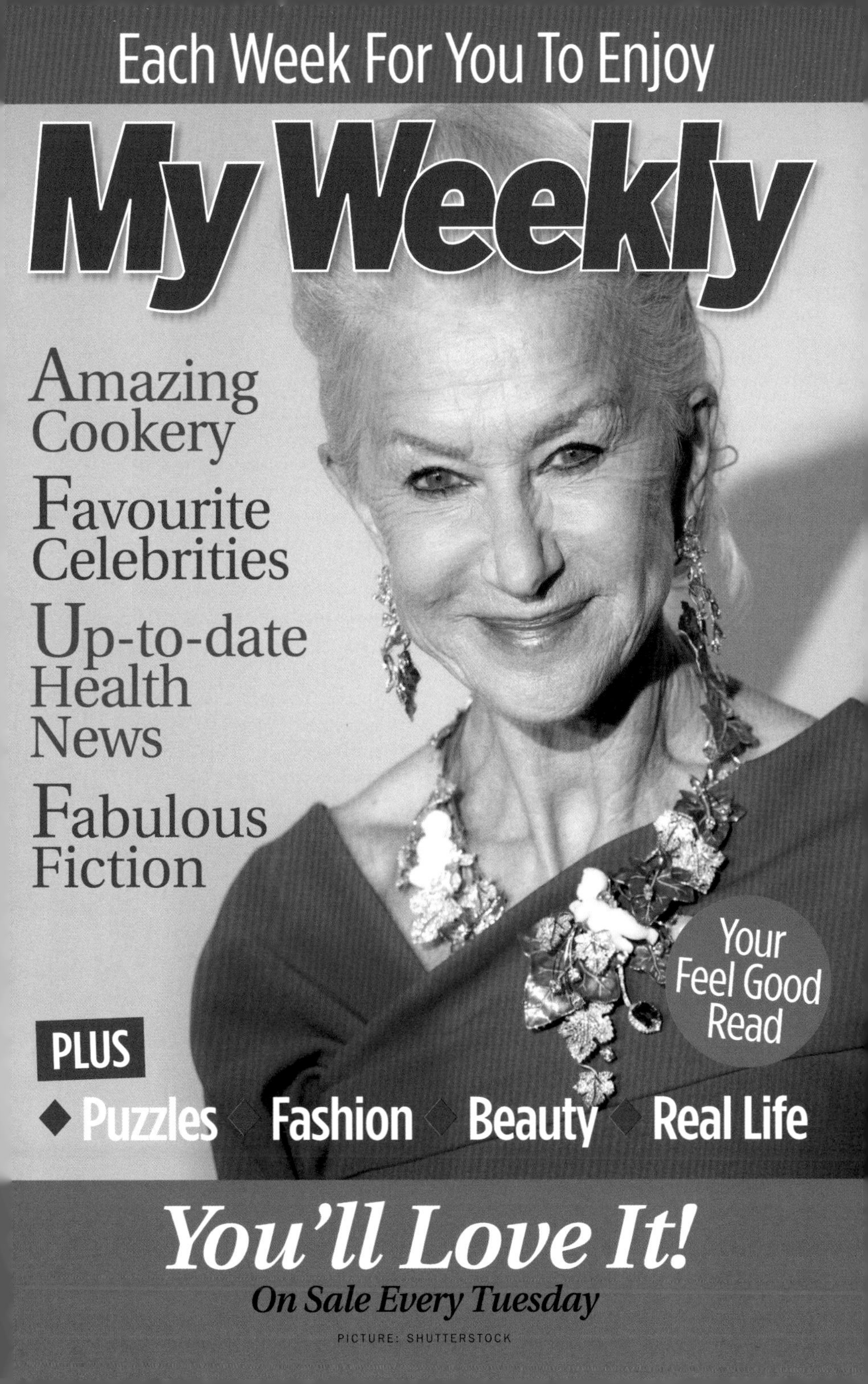

Each Week For You To Enjoy

My Weekly

Amazing
Cookery

Favourite
Celebrities

Up-to-date
Health
News

Fabulous
Fiction

Your
Feel Good
Read

PLUS

◆ Puzzles ◇ Fashion ◇ Beauty ◆ Real Life

You'll Love It!
On Sale Every Tuesday

Finding The Joy

A child's delight in simple things can help put everything else into perspective

By Carrie Hewlett

Waking early Christmas morning, Cassie snuggled deeper under the duvet trying to claw back some semblance of nothingness. Life sucked sometimes. Christmas was about families coming together to celebrate the happiest time of the year. At least, that's what the TV companies would have you believe, shoving cloying sentimentality at you whether you wanted it or not.

All she felt was heartbreak. How could Greg have done that to her?

Watching a romantic Christmas movie on TV the previous night probably hadn't helped her mood.

Glancing at her phone Cassie saw it wasn't yet five a.m. Sam would be awake soon. Her lips curved into a faint smile. He was the one good thing in her life; her amazing six-year-old son. His joie de vivre almost put her to shame. She remembered her dad once telling her that you never forget how to be happy, but sometimes the curtains of life draw a veil across, trying to convince you otherwise.

The first time her dad told her was after she'd broken up with her first boyfriend. Gosh. She must have been about seventeen. A late developer, as her mum said. The tears she'd shed, feeling as though her world had come to an end. But, of course, it hadn't. She'd started dating another boy the following week.

Hearing the sound of running feet hurtling towards her room, she saw the door flung open with careless abandon before Sam leapt onto her bed.

"Mummy! We've got to see if Santa's been, come on…" He pulled on her hand excitement etched on his face.

"OK… OK. Just let me grab my robe," she smiled.

Running downstairs Sam pushed open the lounge door, before whooping in sheer delight.

"Santa did it! It's just what I wanted – look, Mummy, look, a big boy's bike."

"Yay, Santa!"

Cassie felt as excited as Sam did, watching him ooh and ahh over it.

"Can I ride it now?" her son begged.

"Why don't you open your stocking, then grab some breakfast? Once you're dressed, I'll help you wheel it outside."

A little later, with them both wrapped up warm against the cold, frosty air, Cassie steadied Sam as he climbed on. He'd lost his first front tooth that week, so his gappy smile tore at her heartstrings. He was growing up fast. His first tooth. His first bike. Before long it would be his first girlfriend then… She stopped herself. One step at a time.

His grin wavered along with his balance. He'd been adamant in his letter to Santa that he'd wanted a big bike, not a baby one with extra wheels. So that's what she'd bought. But running behind, holding his seat, she wondered if she should have got stabilisers after all. ➜

His grin wavered with his balance. Maybe she should have got stabilisers after all…

There was always a happy ending. You just had to get through the middle bits

Seeing his mouth set into a straight, obstinate line, as he resolutely kept trying to ride without wobbling too much and falling off, she decided that maybe she'd done the right thing.

He'd get there. He always did.

She'd been hoping that it would have been the three of them heading over to her parents' house for Christmas lunch. Her, Greg and Sam. It had taken courage for her to introduce Greg to Sam. And they'd got on OK.

Well… sort of.

But it wasn't to be. It was just a week ago, after nearly a year together, that Greg suddenly dumped her.

Obviously, she'd hidden her heartbreak from Sam, not wanting to ruin Christmas for him. But thinking back, Sam had never really taken to Greg. At the time she'd just assumed that he hadn't want to share her, but maybe he'd sensed that Greg wasn't right for her.

Watching her son's determination to master his balance, Cassie realised that she had fortitude too. Perhaps, some time next year, she'd risk her heart in looking for love again.

Seeing Sam's broad grin as he pelted towards her, his face lit up as bright as the fairy lights on their Christmas tree, she clapped her hands in glee. She was done

crying over what was not meant to be. After all, life was a bit like learning to ride a bike. You'd wobble, fall off, but you'd get back on and keep going. And that's what she would do.

Smelling the mouth-watering aromas of Christmas lunches being cooked, she straightened her shoulders. Maybe the schmaltzy Christmas movies had a point. There was always a happy ending. You just had to get through the middle bits to get there. And maybe it was those middle bits that helped you to grow and appreciate what you already had.

Thankful that her parents lived just round the corner, she smiled.

"Come on, we're going to your gran's for lunch. Let's pack some home-made mince pies, then you can ride over there to show them."

"Yay!" Sam cried. "This is the best Christmas ever!"

Cassie ruffled his head and grinned.

Brain Boosters SOLUTIONS

KRISS KROSS FROM PAGE 30

```
M A S C U L I N E   G
  E     O   E       A
  L     L   W       L   O
  M E D D L E S O M E   D
S   C     I   F   E     Y
C A T E R P I L L A R   S
O   I     O   A   N     S
W A V E   P O S S I B L E
  I   D     H   N     E Y
O U T C R O P   O G R E
  Y   I     A   F   V
    F   G R O U P I E
  U N T I E       L   L
```

CODEWORD FROM PAGE 31
PHRASE: EMMA BUNTON

MISSING LINK FROM PAGE 46

ACROSS: 8 Equal 9 Examine
10 Retreat 11 Error 12 Cartridge
14 Eel 15 Mid 16 Strategic 19 Moral
21 Balance 23 Expense 24 Chess
DOWN: 1 Metric 2 Cultured 3 Else
4 Heated 5 Pavement 6 Pier 7 Petrol
13 Rustling 14 Engineer 15 Member
17 Robber 18 Cheese 20 Rope 22 Lock
SHADED WORD: HELIUM

SUDOKU FROM PAGE 47

7	8	6	9	1	3	2	4	5
2	9	4	7	8	5	6	3	1
1	3	5	4	6	2	9	8	7
6	2	8	3	7	4	1	5	9
4	1	9	5	2	6	8	7	3
3	5	7	1	9	8	4	6	2
8	4	1	2	5	7	3	9	6
9	7	3	6	4	1	5	2	8
5	6	2	8	3	9	7	1	4

WORD WHEEL FROM PAGE 47 The nine-letter word is NEIGHBOUR

MISSING LINK FROM PAGE 53

ACROSS: 8 Emery 9 Leather
10 Amateur 11 Girls 12 Leicester
14 Bin 15 Inn 16 Poisoning 19 Sabre
21 Watcher 23 Dresser 24 Spoke
DOWN: 1 Retail 2 Relation 3 Tyre
4 Floret 5 Kangaroo 6 Char 7 Prison
13 Espresso 14 Brighton 15 Inside
17 Inward 18 Garter 20 Bred 22 Test
SHADED WORD: RUSSET

KRISS KROSS FROM PAGE 62

```
        S C R U F F Y
    S             O
  S H A M E F U L   I
B   A     E     N   S
A   F I R E L I G H T
N   T     C     N O
D     C H E N I L L E   C
L     O   A     T   L   A
E Q U A N I M I T Y     S
A     R   D     A   H   S
D E S T I N A T I O N   O
E     S   E     C   C   C
R   W E A L D   K I N K
```

Brain Boosters SOLUTIONS

CODEWORD FROM PAGE 63
PHRASE: TIGERS

MISSING LINK FROM PAGE 70
ACROSS: 8 Astro 9 Oranges
10 Imposed 11 Thyme 12 Standards
14 Tom 15 Ice 16 Cleansing 19 Towns
21 Strikes 23 Keyhole 24 Dance
DOWN: 1 Habits 2 Stoppage 3 Toes
4 Border 5 Partisan 6 Ugly 7 Esteem
13 Decision 14 Thinking 15 Intake
17 Easter 18 Gospel 20 Ways 22 Ride
SHADED WORD: TINKER

SUDOKO FROM PAGE 71

8	2	7	9	1	5	4	3	6
4	3	5	6	7	2	9	1	8
6	1	9	4	8	3	7	5	2
9	7	3	2	5	6	8	4	1
1	4	8	3	9	7	6	2	5
5	6	2	8	4	1	3	9	7
7	5	4	1	6	9	2	8	3
3	8	1	7	2	4	5	6	9
2	9	6	5	3	8	1	7	4

KRISS KROSS FROM PAGE 80

(Crossword grid with answers including: EVENTING, JUBILATION, LADDISHNESS, INVESTOR, INTRO, PEDAGOGIC, AURA, RISOTTO, DEMOTE)

WORD WHEEL FROM PAGE 71 The nine-letter word is LEGISLATE

CODEWORD FROM PAGE 81
PHRASE: BRITISH AIRWAYS

SUDOKO FROM PAGE 93

2	8	7	5	6	3	1	4	9
5	6	4	9	8	1	7	3	2
9	3	1	7	4	2	5	8	6
7	1	9	3	5	6	8	2	4
6	4	2	8	7	9	3	5	1
3	5	8	2	1	4	6	9	7
4	9	5	6	3	7	2	1	8
1	7	3	4	2	8	9	6	5
8	2	6	1	9	5	4	7	3

WORD WHEEL FROM PAGE 93 The nine-letter word is **COUNTDOWN**

KRISS KROSS FROM PAGE 101

MISSING LINK FROM PAGE 133
ACROSS: 7 Enigma 8 Aerial 9 Plus
10 Mandarin 11 Imagination
14 Composition 18 Delegate 19 Deep
20 Guards 21 Ticket
DOWN: 1 Inflame 2 Ages 3 Gammon
4 Walnut 5 Break out 6 Rapid
12 Geometry 13 Covered 15 Praise
16 Sheets 17 Venue 19 Duck
SHADED WORD: NIPPER

CODEWORD FROM PAGE 113
PHRASE: JACK P. SHEPHERD

SUDOKU FROM PAGE 147

4	9	2	7	8	6	3	1	5
3	1	6	4	2	5	8	7	9
8	5	7	1	9	3	4	6	2
1	4	3	6	5	9	2	8	7
2	6	5	8	7	4	1	9	3
9	7	8	2	3	1	5	4	6
6	2	9	3	1	8	7	5	4
5	3	1	9	4	7	6	2	8
7	8	4	5	6	2	9	3	1

WORD WHEEL FROM PAGE 147 The nine-letter word is **RECTANGLE**

KRISS KROSS FROM PAGE 153

CODEWORD FROM PAGE 161
PHRASE: BAD GIRLS